Marine Aquarium Keeping

Marine Aquarium Keeping

THE SCIENCE, ANIMALS, AND ART

Stephen Spotte

Director of Aquariums
Aquarium Systems, Inc.
Eastlake, Ohio

A WILEY-INTERSCIENCE PUBLICATION

JOHN WILEY & SONS, New York · London · Sydney · Toronto

Published by John Wiley & Sons, Inc.

Library of Congress Cataloging in Publication Data:

Spotte, Stephen
Marine aquarium keeping.

"A Wiley-Interscience publication."
Bibliography: p.
1. Marine aquariums. I. Title.

SF457.1.S66   639'.34   73–4425
ISBN 0–471–81759–7
Printed in the United States of America

10 9 8 7 6 5 4 3

FOR CAROL

Preface

〜〜〜〜〜

As I write this sentence waves are breaking in frothy madness on the beach outside my window. The tail end of a winterstorm brings a brown and broken sea here to the edge of the land. Tomorrow its surface will be placid and the waves will break differently, although in the ancient structure of things such differences do not account for much. Ocean waves are still changeless in the gradually changing order of the universe.

Stability is the very essence of the sea. Its chemical composition hardly differs from day to day, year to year, century to century. Only the living things that drift and swim have diversified, mute testimony to the positive forces of stable environments.

The water is everything. Because sea water was the medium in which life evolved we are all, in a sense, self-contained oceans. Our blood has a composition reminiscent of the sea. All life, in fact, consists of variations on a single theme. You could almost say that nature took sea water, an old, original product, and repackaged it in different ways, some to be called fish, others trees, and still others men.

But if the sea is the stablest of environments, a marine aquarium is perhaps the most unstable. Without winds and surf, global currents, and the cleansing activities of uncountable microorganisms an aquarium is pathetically isolated and vulnerable. And as confinement alters the chemistry of the water the captive animals, unaccustomed to sudden changes throughout their long evolution, will weaken and die.

In the following pages I describe some of the commonly kept marine creatures and even explain how to exhibit them more attractively. Yet in the long run such matters are of minor importance. How well you control the inevitable changes taking place in the sea water will determine whether the aquarium succeeds or fails. The water, you see, is everything. It's as simple as that.

STEPHEN SPOTTE

Brooklyn, New York
January 1973

Acknowledgments

No book of information is written in a vacuum. I am especially indebted to three people who read the entire manuscript and offered many valuable suggestions: Dr. James W. Atz of The American Museum of Natural History, Mr. John M. King of Aquarium Systems, Inc., and Mr. H. Douglas Kemper, Jr., of the New York Aquarium. The concepts presented in the section in Chapter 3 that deals with ultraviolet irradiation are the original work of Mr. Sidney Ellner of Ultraviolet Purification Systems, Inc., and Dr. Glenn L. Hoffman of the U. S. Department of the Interior, Eastern Fish Disease Laboratory; any mistakes in mathematics or interpretation are mine. Dr. George D. Ruggieri, S.J., of the Osborn Laboratories of Marine Science read Chapter 10.

My gratitude is extended to those authors, artists, and photographers who let me reprint portions of their work. They are cited by name under Credits.

Finally, thanks must go to my editor Mr. Alan W. Frankenfield of John Wiley & Sons for his encouragement throughout the preparation of the book (and also the use of his swimming pool). The fine illustrations are the painstaking work of Frances McKittrick Watkins. Typing of the manuscript was ably handled by Mrs. Alice Kemper.

S. S.

Contents

〰〰〰

The Science

Chapter One

〰〰〰〰〰

Sea Water

1.1 COMPOSITION

Every substance in the universe is composed of *matter*. The paper on which these words are printed is matter. So are your eyes and the fingers you use to turn the pages. Matter is made up of smaller constituents known as *molecules*. These are composed of even smaller things called *elements*, which in turn are made of *atoms*. For our discussions an atom is the end of the line; there need be nothing smaller.

Some atoms have tiny electrical charges, either positive or negative. Electrically charged atoms are referred to as *ions*. Ions can combine to form molecules of compounds called *salts*. The formula below illustrates this principle in the symbolic language of chemists; Figure 1 shows it diagrammatically.

$$Na^+ + Cl^- \rightleftharpoons NaCl.$$

Sea water is composed mainly of salts, of which there are many kinds. Table salt, or plain sodium chloride, is the most common. Epsom salt (magnesium sulfate) and gypsum (calcium sulfate) are two more. The ionic composition of sea water is given in Table 1.

1.2 NATURAL SEA WATER

Although the elements and salts found in the sea are inorganic and therefore nonliving, it is wiser for us to consider sea water in its natural state as a

Table 1　Composition of Sea Water

Constituent	Concentration (ppm)
Chloride	18,980
Sodium	10,560
Sulfate	2,560
Magnesium	1,272
Calcium	400
Potassium	380
Bicarbonate	142
Bromide	65
Strontium	13
Boron	4.6
Fluoride	1.4
Rubidium	0.2
Aluminum	0.16–1.9
Lithium	0.1
Barium	0.05
Iodide	0.05
Silicate	0.04–8.6
Nitrogen	0.03–0.9
Zinc	0.005–0.014
Lead	0.004–0.005
Selenium	0.004
Arsenic	0.003–0.024
Copper	0.001–0.09
Tin	0.003
Iron	0.002–0.02
Cesium	~0.002
Manganese	0.001
Phosphorous	0.001–0.10
Thorium	$\leqslant 0.0005$
Mercury	0.0003
Uranium	0.00015–0.0016
Cobalt	0.0001
Nickel	0.0001–0.0005
Radium	8×10^{-11}
Beryllium	. . .
Cadmium	. . .
Chromium	. . .
Titanium	Trace

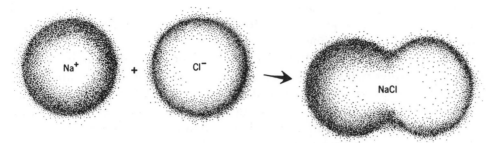

Figure 1   A sodium ion and a chloride ion combine to form a molecule of sodium chloride.

living substance. This makes it easier to understand why it must be treated in certain ways before use in the aquarium.

When you scoop up water from the surface of the ocean, you are seldom aware that it teems with life because most of the organisms are microscopic and invisible to the naked eye. Nevertheless, any sample of sea water, no matter how clear it looks, will contain thousands of simple one-celled animals and plants called *plankton* by oceanographers. Literally translated, this term means wanderer. A random sampling of planktonic organisms, as seen through a microscope, is shown in Figure 2.

The plankton immediately start altering the chemical composition of the newly collected water. The tiny animals prey on one another and on the plants, use up the oxygen, and give off carbon dioxide. Perhaps most important, they start to die, and their decaying remains poison the water, making it unfit to sustain other forms of life. In water taken at certain times of the year when plankton are most abundant, these changes may occur so rapidly that the water actually gives off an odor of decay after only a few hours in storage.

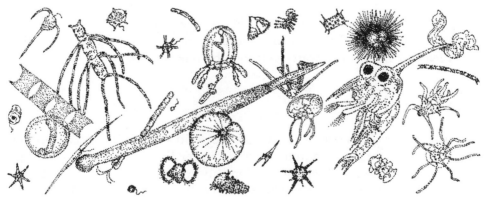

Figure 2   Plankton.

To prevent possible poisoning of your aquarium, let newly collected sea water stand in a darkened room (or in lightproof containers) for at least three weeks. During this time the containers should be at room temperature.

In the course of these three weeks the biological and chemical constituents of the water will stabilize. Some species of plankton will disappear and among those that are left some will increase in number and others will decrease until the population finally stabilizes. The chemistry of the water will also reach an equilibrium as the plant and animal populations come into balance. The poisons that were initially produced (mainly ammonia) will have been biologically altered to less toxic states. The water is now fit to use.

HOW TO COLLECT NATURAL SEA WATER

1. Collect only offshore water. Inshore water is often polluted or heavily laden with silt and bacteria. It may also be too dilute after periods of heavy rainfall.
2. Use inert containers for collecting and storing sea water. Do not use galvanized buckets or anything with copper, brass, or bronze fittings. The zinc in the galvanizing and the copper in brass and bronze are highly toxic to marine life.
3. Collect upcurrent from the boat to be sure that no leaking oil or gasoline from the engine contaminates the water.
4. Keep the containers tightly sealed during storage. This keeps out tobacco smoke, insecticides, paint fumes, and other airborne contaminants. Plastic "jerry cans" make ideal storage units. The outside of the cans should be labeled with a crayon or wax pencil to show the date of collection (Figure 3).
5. Collect after periods of calm. After storms or rough weather even offshore seas are often turbid.

When the water has been sufficiently aged, siphon the silt from the bottoms of the cans. Drop an airstone into each can and aerate it mildly for at least 12 hours. The water will then be ready to use.

1.3 SYNTHETIC SEA WATER

A marine aquarium is not, as many imagine, a little slice of the ocean brought indoors. If it were, marine animals could never live in synthetic sea water. As its name implies, synthetic sea water only superficially resembles the real stuff, yet it works just as well. This is indeed fortunate for inland hobbyists.

A good quality synthetic sea water contains only those substances that are essential to marine animals for normal growth and reproduction. The

Figure 3   Plastic jerry can with a tag showing when the sea water was collected.

rest are omitted, as seen by comparing Tables 1 and 2. Natural sea water, if you remember, contains many elements, but this is not to say marine animals need all of them. Far from it. Many of the *trace elements* (those present in tiny amounts) are probably of no use whatever to the sea's creatures, although a few, such as copper, zinc, silicon, and vanadium are known to be important. Synthetic sea water, then, is far less complex than ocean water because it offers the animals what they basically need and no more.

Most brands of synthetic sea water are packaged in plastic bags and mixed with regular tap water (Figure 4). Some are mixed in a single step, whereas others require two or more steps. The important thing is to follow the instructions on the package carefully and to mix the salts in a separate container—not the aquarium tank.

Plastic jerry cans are again ideally suited to small batches (5 gal or less). For larger amounts a plastic garbage can is recommended. Be sure it is clean inside and has a tight-fitting lid. Set the can on two cinder blocks so that the finished water can be siphoned into smaller containers and carried to the aquarium tank. It is always wise to check the exact volume of the can and mark it (in 5-gal increments) on the outside with a wax pencil or crayon, as illustrated in Figure 5.

The tap water used in hydration should be in the temperature range of 70 to 80 F (21–26 C). After adding the water place an airstone in the container, put the lid on, and aerate the solution mildly for at least 24 hours before use.

Table 2   Composition of a Synthetic Sea Salt Mix (INSTANT OCEAN® Synthetic Sea Salts)

Constituent	Concentration (ppm)
Chloride	18,400
Sodium	10,200
Sulfate	2,500
Magnesium	1,200
Calcium	370
Potassium	370
Bicarbonate	140
Boric acid	25
Bromide	20
Strontium	8
Silicate	3
Phosphate	1
Manganese	1
Molybdate	0.7
Thiosulfate	0.4
Lithium	0.2
Rubidium	0.1
Iodide	0.07
EDTA	0.05
Aluminium	0.04
Zinc	0.02
Vanadium	0.02
Cobalt	0.01
Iron	0.01
Copper	0.003

Most synthetic sea waters are cloudy at first until all the components have dissolved. The solution should not be used until it turns clear.

Figure 4   A synthetic sea salt mix.

Figure 5   A clean plastic garbage can is useful for mixing large batches of synthetic sea water. This one is marked in five-gallon increments with a wax pencil and set on cinder blocks for easy drainage.

1.4 SALT CONTENT

The total amount of salts in solution can be measured as salinity or specific gravity, although the latter is more commonly used by marine aquarists.

Salinity is a weight relationship. By definition, salinity is the total amount of solid material in grams (g) contained in one kilogram (kg) of sea water after various chemical reactions have taken place. Grams per kilogram means the same as parts per thousand (ppt), since there are 1000 grams in a single kilogram. One gram per kilogram, in other words, would be 1 ppt; 34 g/kg—the normal salinity of sea water—would be 34 ppt. Parts per thousand is sometimes written with the symbol ‰.

Specific gravity is a ratio. Specifically, it is the ratio of the weight of a given volume of sea water to the weight of an equal volume of distilled water. Because sea water is heavier, the ratio must be greater than 1. Distilled water has a specific gravity of 1.000; normal strength sea water is 1.025.

All this leads to an obvious question: what are the natural limits governing the salt content of different waters? A summary is given in Table 3.

Table 3   Classification of Salt Content

Type of Water	Salinity (‰)	Specific Gravity
Fresh	<0.5	1.000
Brackish	0.5–30.0	1.000 –1.0220
Sea	30.0–37.0	1.0220–1.0275
Metahaline	>37.0	>1.0275

Fresh water and sea water should need no additional explanation. *Brackish* water is common in estuaries or inshore areas, where runoff from the land lowers the salt content. Tidal marshes, for instance, are classed as brackish. *Metahaline* waters include salt lakes and tropical lagoons in which limited circulation and high surface evaporation combine to concentrate the salts.

Chapter Two

≋≋≋≋≋≋

Setting Up

2.1   THE AQUARIUM TANK

Four things must be considered before buying an aquarium tank and setting
it up.

SIZE

No marine aquarium should be smaller than 20 gallons. Larger tanks support
life better than small ones, mostly because aquarists are less likely to overcrowd them with too many animals. A small tank, in other words, suffers
more often from the "one-fish-too-many" syndrome.

CONSTRUCTION

The aquarium tank should be constructed entirely of glass. Older style tanks
with metal frames are unsuitable because inevitably the frame will rust,
ugly brown spots will form on the outside, and the life of the tank itself will
be shortened.

The modern all-glass tank consists of five pieces of glass: four sides and
a bottom. They are held together with a silicone sealant, which is inert and
more pliable than old-style aquarium cement. Although an all-glass tank is
simple to build, it is recommended that the beginning aquarist buy a ready-
made model. By doing so he is guaranteed that standard accessories will fit
and that the tank will not leak.

Figure 6   All-glass aquarium tank (high model).

STYLE

Tanks come in two basic styles: high and low. The high tank, as shown in Figure 6, has a greater vertical height but a reduced surface area, whereas the low tank is the opposite; it has a low vertical profile and greater surface area (Figure 7). The low is the better of the two because surface area is much more important than height (or water depth, if you prefer), as will be shown later.

LOCATION

Do not set up the aquarium in front of a window in direct sunlight or heavy growths of algae will occur. Neither should the aquarium be placed in a

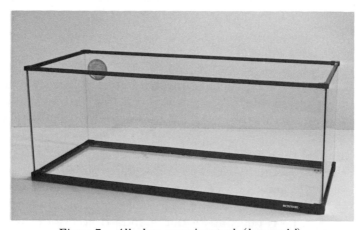

Figure 7   All-glass aquarium tank (low model).

cold draft, such as in a hallway entrance. Warm air is just as harmful and the tank should stand a good distance from the nearest radiator or hot-air louver. The room should be of nearly constant temperature year-round. It should also be a room frequented by people; otherwise the fish will develop a sensitivity to any movement outside the tank and will hide when you come near.

Once you have decided on the right room, consider the support for the tank. Sea water weighs about 8.5 lb/gal; therefore, a 20-gal tank will contain at least 170 lb of water when full.   The tank itself will add to the weight, as will the stand and other accessories. A good, sturdy support is obviously mandatory. For exceptionally large tanks also check the supporting structure under the floor. A friend of mine once built a 100-gal marine aquarium of plywood and glass. He was an expert aquarist and thought of everything, right down to the final detail; everything, that is, except the total weight. He made the mistake of putting the aquarium in his study on the second floor instead of in the game room in the basement, where the floor was solid concrete. On arriving home from work one evening he found a large hole in the ceiling of his living room and the room itself littered from end to end with broken glass, plaster, gravel, puddles of water, and dead fish.

2.2   THE SUBGRAVEL FILTER

FUNCTION

The subgravel filter is a perforated plastic plate that rests on the bottom of the tank, as shown in Figure 8. It looks simple enough, and it is, but its function is vital to the internal workings of the aquarium. The subgravel filter serves as a support for the gravel, allowing water to circulate underneath. Without it stagnant areas would develop in the gravel and would result in the build-up of noxious substances like hydrogen sulfide, methane, and carbon dioxide. The ultimate effect, of course, would be the quick demise of your animals.

SIZE

Select a subgravel filter that covers the entire bottom of the aquarium tank.

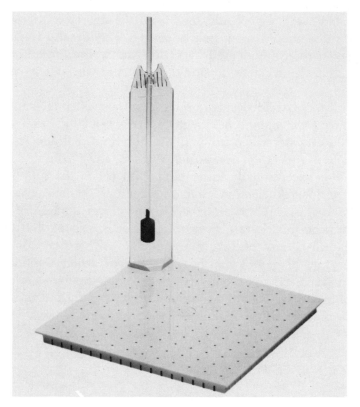

Figure 8   Subgravel filter plate with a corner airlift pump.

2.3   THE GRAVEL

The nature of the gravel is one of the most important aspects of maintaining a successful marine aquarium. These four factors must be considered in the selection of this material.

COMPOSITION

If you were keeping freshwater fishes, the composition of the gravel would not be too important, but in marine aquariums it must be *calcareous* (containing calcium). Four kinds are available: limestone, crushed oyster shell, coral rock, and dolomite (Figure 9). The first is composed entirely of calcium carbonate ($CaCO_3$) and is the least desirable. The last three contain mostly calcium carbonate but also a sizable amount of magnesium carbonate ($MgCO_3$). This makes them better filter media for marine aquariums. Dolomite, a form of ancient limestone, contains half and half calcium carbonate and magnesium carbonate.

Crushed oyster shell can be obtained at feed stores, where it is sold for

Figure 9   The three most desirable filter media for a marine aquarium are (left *to* right): *crushed coral rock, crushed oyster shell, and dolomite.*

poultry grit. Coral gravel (i.e., crushed coral rock) is often unavailable to northern aquarists. Dolomite can sometimes be purchased from quarries. Any of these materials is suitable.

The gravel must also be *graded;* that is, the grains must be of uniform size. Gravels sold in aquarium supply stores are always graded, but if you buy elsewhere they may not be.

SHAPE

As shown in Figure 10, gravel should be rough and angular, not smooth and round. The sharp edges make it a better filter medium, as explained in more detail in Chapter 3.

SIZE

Gravel grains $\frac{3}{16}$ in. (2–5 mm) work best.

QUANTITY

Get enough gravel to make a layer 3 in. deep on top of the subgravel filter. Less than this amount reduces the filtering capacity of the tank.

Figure 10   Closeup photograph of dolomite grains showing the angularity. Rough, angular gravels are preferable to smooth, rounded types.

2.4   THE OUTSIDE FILTER

The outside filter can be considered as auxiliary filtration because its functions are not so vital as those of the subgravel filter. Nevertheless, it is a useful piece of equipment and any marine aquarium functions better with one.

THE FILTER UNIT

The filter unit, as seen in Figure 11, consists of a plastic compartment that hangs on the outside of the aquarium. It can be purchased at most aquarium supply stores. Do not buy what is known as a "power filter," with its special pump (see Chapter 10, Section 9). A simple outside filter unit powered by air is more than adequate.

ACTIVATED CARBON

Activated carbon, or "charcoal," is one of two filter media that are put into the case. When you buy it, be sure it comes completely sealed in a plastic bag. Material packaged in cardboard is unsuitable because the carbon granules readily adsorb substances from the air as well as from the water in the aquarium. If it has not been packaged in the airtight container, it may

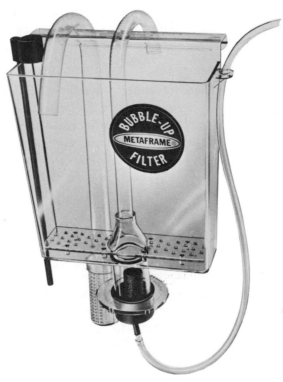

Figure 11   Outside filter unit.

Figure 12   The two media that go into an outside filter are filter fiber (left) *and activated carbon, or "charcoal"* (right).

15

have picked up poisonous substances like paint fumes, tobacco smoke, or insecticides, and concentrated them.

FILTER FIBER

Filter fiber is a general term for spun polyester fibers, also available at aquarium supply stores. Be sure to specify polyester, as opposed to spun glass ("angel hair"), because the glass may lacerate the gills of your fishes if it accidently gets into the water of the tank. Activated carbon and filter fiber are shown in Figure 12.

2.5   THE AIR-FLOW SYSTEM

AIR COMPRESSOR

The air compressor (sometimes called an "air pump") must be of good quality. Your animals depend on a constant flow of air into the water; without it they quickly die, so don't rely on a cheap one. Suitable compressors are available at aquarium supply stores for less than 20 dollars. "Vibrator" and "piston" are the two types available. Either is suitable (Figures 13 and 14).

Figure 13   Vibrator-type air compressor.

Figure 14   Piston-type air compressor.

AIR-LINE TUBING

The tubing from the air compressor to the aquarium tank should be standard size ($\frac{3}{16}$-in. inside diameter) and manufactured from clear polethylene. It can also be bought at aquarium supply stores.

GANG VALVE

A gang valve is essential in aquarium tanks with more than one filter unit. The valve splits the flow of air coming from the compressor and distributes it to the filters, as shown in Figure 15. Gang valves are available at aquarium supply stores.

Figure 15   Gang valves.

AIRLIFT PUMPS

Airlift pumps are built right into both the outside filter and the subgravel filter. All you need to do is hook them into the compressor with the air-line tubing.

On the subgravel filter the air-line tubing slips over the end of the smaller of the two vertical tubes, as shown in Figure 16. Pressure from the compressor forces air through the tubing, down through the slender part of the airlift, across the connecting isthmus, and into an airstone inside the larger tube (called the *lift tube*). The airstone diffuses the air into many fine bubbles, which mix with water inside the lift tube. The air-water mixture is lighter than water alone and so it rises. It is not "lifted" in the strict sense of the word but is "displaced" upward. The lighter air-water mixture then spills out of the end of the lift tube and is replaced by water moving in from underneath the subgravel filter.

The outside filter has two tubes, as shown in Figure 11. Water enters the unit from the aquarium tank through the siphon tube and passes through the filter fiber and activated carbon, then down through a perforated plate in the bottom. It is airlifted from underneath the plate through a lift tube and back into the aquarium. The airstone disperses the air, making the airlift more efficient. A continuous flow through the siphon can be kept up because water in the filter is always lower than in the tank.

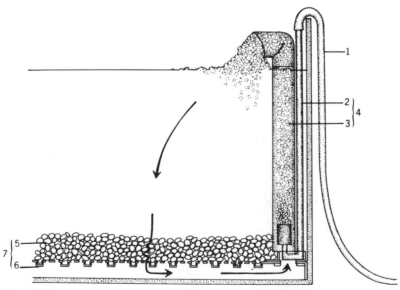

Figure 16   Airlift pump in operation: (1) air-line tubing; (2) connecting tube; (3) lift pipe; (4) airlift pump; (5) gravel; (6) subgravel filter plate; (7) filter bed. Arrows show the flow of water.

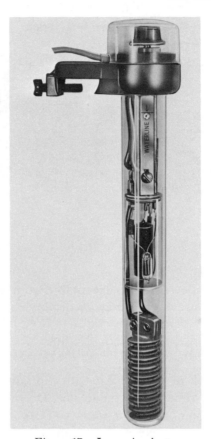

Figure 17   Immersion heater.

2.6   THE HEATER

The heater, like the compressor, must be a well-made piece of equipment, especially if the temperature of the room fluctuates. The type used in aquarium keeping is called an *immersion heater* (Figure 17). Good ones can be purchased at aquarium supply stores. Be sure to give the dealer the dimensions of your tank so that he can supply the right size. A good rule of thumb is two watts per gallon of water to be heated.

2.7   THE REFLECTOR

A marine aquarium should be covered at all times. A cover reduces surface evaporation and helps keep the salt content at the same concentration. It also keeps the fishes from jumping out.

Reflectors, or hoods, for marine aquariums should be made of plastic and stainless steel; otherwise the various parts will corrode (Figure 18). The fixtures inside determine whether the unit will take incandescent bulbs

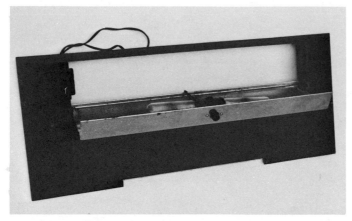

Figure 18   Reflector, or hood.

or fluorescent tubes. Either is acceptable from a health standpoint. Incandes‑cent lighting, however, is better for displaying the true colors of the animals.

2.8   PROCEDURE FOR SETTING UP

1. Set the tank in place, fill it with tap water, and check for leaks. If the tank leaks, return it to the dealer. Do not attempt to patch it yourself.
2. Dip or siphon out all the water you can, then tip the tank and pour out the last little bit. Never try to lift or tip a tank with even a couple of gallons of water in it because you could crack the glass. An aquarium, when filled, should be considered a permanent installation.
3. Assemble the subgravel filter and place it in the tank.
4. New gravel is dusty and must be washed. Put some into a clean bucket or dishpan and hold it under running tap water. Stir the gravel vigorously with your hands, as shown in Figure 19, until the water flowing over the edges of the pan turns clear.
5. Drain off all the water and empty the gravel into the tank. If a signifi‑cant amount of tap water should get into the tank with the gravel, it will dilute the sea water when you add it later.
6. Clean all the gravel in this manner. When finished, smooth it evenly over the subgravel filter with your hand.
7. Assemble the outside filter according to the instructions on the package. Hang it on the back of the tank or on one of the ends.
8. The activated carbon, like the gravel, is dusty at first. This dust floats, and if any gets into the tank it will leave a ring around the edge and your aquarium will look like a dirty bathtub. Wash enough to fill the case of the outside filter three-fourths full. Put the remainder back in the plastic bag and seal it up with a rubber band. Remember, it is import‑ant that no air be allowed to contaminate the carbon.

Figure 19   When washing gravel, put it in a bucket and hold it under running tap water until the water turns clear.

9. Fill the space remaining in the case with filter fiber. It should be packed in moderately tight. If it is too loose, it will allow particles to pass through; if too tight, it will restrict water flow. New filter fiber does not need washing.
10. Set the air compressor in its permanent spot.
11. Attach one end of the air-line tubing to the outlet on the compressor and run the tubing to where the gang valve is to be attached.
12. Cut the tubing and attach it to one of the side stems of the valve.
13. Hook up the subgravel filter and the outside filter to other stems.
14. Add the sea water. Fill the tank to about two inches from the top. When filling, pour the water into a bowl set on the bottom (Figure 20). This prevents unnecessary splashing and stirring of the gravel.
15. Plug in the compressor. The flow of air will start the subgravel filter bubbling, but the siphon on the outside filter may have to be started manually. This depends on the design of the outside filter unit.
16. When both filters are running, adjust the gang valve so that the flow from each is about the same. The flow of water through the filters is called the *turnover rate*, and it is measured in terms of the volume of water discharged through an airlift. Ideally, the total discharge from all the airlifts should equal a rate of one gallon per square foot of surface area of the tank per minute (1 gpm/ft^2).

Figure 20   Pour the water into a bowl to prevent stirring up the gravel once it has been leveled.

EXAMPLE.   The tank is 12 in. wide and 30 in. long. In feet, this is $1 \times 2.5 = 2.5$ ft.^{2} By holding a measuring cup under the discharge from an airlift we see that it can fill four cups in 10 sec. Four cups = 1 qt, which is 0.25 gal. If the airlift can fill 0.25 gal in 10 sec, it can fill $0.25 \times 6 = 1.5$ gal in 60 sec. Therefore

$$\frac{1.5 \text{ gal}}{2.5 \text{ ft}^2} = \frac{x \text{ gal}}{1 \text{ ft}^2}.$$

Solving for x, we get

$$2.5x = 1.5$$

$$x = 0.6 \text{ gpm/ft}^2.$$

This means that the discharge from the other airlift (if there are two) should be about 0.4 gpm/ft^2. Understand that calculating turnover rate merely gives you an accurate starting point. After a few days your practiced eye will enable you to make adjustments in the flow of water without having to measure it.

17. Read the instructions that come with the heater and put it in place. Most heaters have indicator lights and thermostats that can be set manually. Adjust the heater so that the light just shuts off. It should then keep the tank at room temperature. If you want it warmer, set the thermostat so that the light comes on again and shut it off when the desired temperature has been reached. For tropical fishes and invertebrates the ideal temperature is about 70 to 73 F (21–23 C). Fahrenheit to centigrade conversions are given in Table 4; centigrade to Fahrenheit conversions in Table 5.

18. Set the reflector in place. Allow the water to circulate through the filters for 24 hours before adding the animals.

Table 4   Temperature Conversions

Fahrenheit	to	Centigrade	Fahrenheit	to	Centigrade
86		30.0	58		14.4
85		29.4	57		13.9
84		28.9	56		13.3
83		28.3	55		12.8
82		27.8	54		12.2
81		27.2	53		11.7
80		26.7	52		11.1
79		26.1	51		10.6
78		25.6	50		10.0
77		25.0	49		9.4
76		24.4	48		8.9
75		23.9	47		8.3
74		23.3	46		7.8
73		22.8	45		7.2
72		22.2	44		6.7
71		21.7	43		6.1
70		21.1	42		5.6
69		20.6	41		5.0
68		20.0	40		4.4
67		19.4	39		3.9
66		18.9	38		3.3
65		18.3	37		2.8
64		17.8	36		2.2
63		17.2	35		1.7
62		16.7	34		1.1
61		16.1	33		0.6
60		15.6	32		0.0
59		15.0			

Table 5   Temperature Conversions

Centigrade	to	Fahrenheit	Centigrade	to	Fahrenheit
30		86.0	14		57.2
29		84.2	13		55.4
28		82.4	12		53.6
27		80.6	11		51.8
26		78.8	10		50.0
25		77.0	9		48.2
24		75.2	8		46.4
23		73.4	7		44.6
22		71.6	6		42.8
21		69.8	5		41.0
20		68.0	4		39.2
19		66.2	3		37.4
18		64.4	2		35.6
17		62.6	1		33.8
16		60.8	0		32.0
15		59.0			

Chapter Three

Filtration

3.1 PURPOSE OF FILTRATION

Harmful and potentially harmful substances may gradually accumulate in aquarium water, eventually poisoning the animals. Only filtration can keep this from happening. For our purposes *filtration* can be defined as the removal of unwanted substances from water. A successful aquarist uses three types: biological, mechanical, and chemical, among which the first is the most important.

3.2 BIOLOGICAL FILTRATION

Biological filtration is invisible. You can't see it happening and, unless you are properly equipped, you can't even measure its effects. Yet this single process is the difference between success or failure, and the aquarist who does not take the time to understand its workings is doomed to watch an endless procession of dying fishes passing through his tank.

Biological filtration is solely the work of bacteria attached to the surfaces of the gravel. The gravel and the subgravel filter together constitute the *filter bed*, as shown in Figure 16. Bacteria reach the filter bed by various means: the air, the animals themselves, the food you feed to the animals, even your hands as you work in the tank. As the water ages, their numbers increase until the gravel teems with them. Then, and only then, does your aquarium truly function well. We can define *biological filtration* as the removal of unwanted substances, primarily ammonia, from the water by bacteria.

It would be natural to ask at this point where the ammonia comes from. The answer is, two sources: as an end product from decaying organic matter (dead animals and plants, uneaten food, etc.) and the living animals themselves. Ammonia is one of the primary excretory products of marine animals.

AMMONIFICATION

Besides ammonia, marine animals excrete a variety of organic compounds into the water. An *organic compound* is any chemical substance containing the element carbon. Organic matter can be broken down into its simpler components and, ultimately, into its original basic elements, and this is what the first stage in biological filtration does. The other two stages are nitrification and denitrification. Biological filtration is shown diagrammatically in Figure 21.

Ammonification is the decomposition, or "mineralization," of the organic to the inorganic which produces ammonia and other simple substances. Ordinary decay is the best example. Because ammonia is the primary product, the process is named for it: the production of ammonia (Figure 21).

Ammonification is accomplished by a special group of bacteria in the aquarium gravel. Their source of energy is organic matter and they are called *heterotrophic bacteria*. As shown in Figure 21, heterotrophs decompose organic substances into ammonia and other compounds. At this point another group takes over.

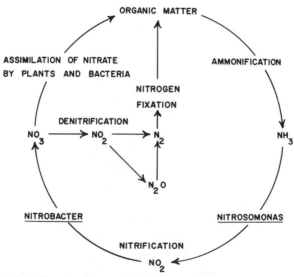

Figure 21   Biological filtration (ammonification, nitrification, and denitrification).

It is especially fortunate for the aquarist that one particular group of bacteria becomes established in the filter bed. The *nitrifying bacteria* are able to use ammonia as a source of food, thereby ridding the water of it. In a process known as *nitrification* nitrifying bacteria detoxify ammonia in two steps. First one group (*Nitrosomonas*) converts it to a somewhat less poisonous substance, nitrite (NO_2^-). The second step converts nitrite to nitrate (NO_3^-), which is much less toxic. This is accomplished by bacteria in the genus *Nitrobacter*. Nitrification is described diagrammatically in Figure 21. As you can see, ammonia, nitrite, and nitrate are all inorganic compounds. Bacteria such as nitrifiers that are able to use inorganic substances as energy sources are called *autotrophic bacteria*.

Nitrification is self-sustaining as long as environmental conditions remain suitable for the growth of bacteria. Aquarium animals release a continuous stream of organic matter and ammonia into the water as they eat and grow. With a steady food supply both groups of bacteria—the heterotrophs and the autotrophs—can carry out their functions indefinitely.

DENITRIFICATION

The third stage in biological filtration is *denitrification*. In this process the nitrite and nitrate produced during nitrification are chemically reduced by denitrifying bacteria to nitrous oxide (N_2O) or to molecular nitrogen (N_2), as also shown in Figure 21. Without denitrification the nitrate level could increase dangerously. Denitrification is also an autotrophic process.

CARRYING CAPACITY

More captive marine animals die from the results of overcrowding than from any other combination of factors. Unfortunately, no one has yet devised a foolproof formula for determining the animal load that an aquarium tank of given dimensions can accommodate. The old simple standby of freshwater aquarists—one inch of fish per gallon of water—fails to take into account the surface area of the filter bed, which is much more important in marine aquariums than volume of water.

At the other extreme some Japanese scientists have worked out a complex formula that includes, among other factors, grain size of the gravel, dissolved oxygen, and weight of the food going into the aquarium daily. This is obviously impractical for the hobbyist.

The amount of animals an aquarium can safely hold is its *carrying capacity*. In marine aquariums *maximum carrying capacity is three inches of animal (fish or invertebrate) per square foot of filter bed surface area*. This relationship holds only under the following conditions: grain size of the gravel is $\frac{3}{16}$ in. (2–5 mm), turnover rate is a minimum of 1 gpm/ft², minimum depth of the filter bed is 3 in., and the animals are never overfed.

EXAMPLE.   Width of filter bed = 12 in.
            Length of filter bed = 30 in.
            In square feet,
                1 ft × 2.5 ft   = 2.5 ft².
            At 3 in. of animal per square foot of filter bed,
                3 × 2.5 = 7.5 in. of animal

CONDITIONING THE FILTER BED

The first two weeks are critical for a new aquarium. During this time the amount of ammonia is likely to rise because not enough nitrifying bacteria have established themselves in the gravel to convert it. Once the bacterial population has stabilized with a steady input of food in the form of ammonia and organic matter the aquarium is *conditioned*.

The nitrification process is shown graphically in Figure 22. Ammonia "peaks out," usually within two weeks, unless the aquarium tank is over-crowded. The fall in the ammonia level is quickly followed by a "peaking out" of nitrite. Throughout, nitrate slowly but steadily rises, finally stabilizing at a point below the 20-ppm level. The curves shown are idealized, and many variations will be found under actual aquarium conditions.

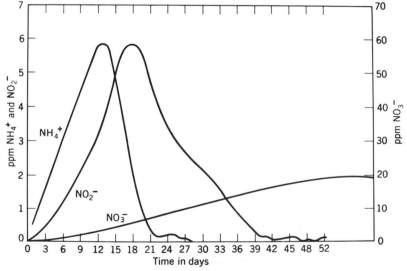

Figure 22   Idealized nitrification curve for a warm-water marine aquarium.

Obviously it is desirable to speed up the conditioning process. The best way is to take some gravel from an already conditioned filter and add it to yours. This old gravel will be teeming with microorganisms if the aquarium is healthy and will rapidly spread viable bacteria throughout your new filter bed. The conditioning process can be cut in half by using this method; that is, if your tank is not overcrowded.

If no one around has a conditioned marine aquarium from which to lend you gravel, there are two other methods to get your aquarium off to a good start—not so fast but just as safe.

Method 1.   Buy some inexpensive, hardy animals and add them to the tank all at once. Leave them for at least two weeks, feeding them regularly to assure a steady input of ammonia. After this time take them out and add a slightly smaller quantity of the animals you intend to keep. Some animals, like groupers, are particularly insensitive to ammonia at sublethal concentrations. They will condition your aquarium and eliminate the risk of jeopardizing more valuable display specimens during the touchy conditioning period.

Method 2.   Add your animals a few at a time instead of all at once. In small aquarium tanks add them one at a time, a week apart. This gives the filter bed ample time to adjust to each new increase in ammonia. This is the recommended method, since it doesn't risk wasting the life of an animal, no matter how common or inexpensive it may be.

As a rule of thumb a new aquarium can be considered safe for animals (though it is not yet completely conditioned) when the total ammonia level has fallen to less than 0.1 ppm and the nitrite has peaked.

BACTERIA AND COMMON SENSE

The bacteria at work in aquariums are marvelous organisms. They make the aquarist's work much easier, but they can't compensate for his mistakes. The worst mistakes you can make are to overcrowd the animals, overfeed them, and not remove them promptly if they die. Almost as serious is shutting off the air supply to the subgravel filter.

At the beginning of this chapter I stated that harmful and "potentially harmful" substances gradually accumulate in aquarium water. Ammonia is directly harmful, and the potentially harmful substances include bits of organic matter lying about, such as a dead fish or a piece of uneaten food. These objects all decay, and when they do one of the end products is ammonia. The heterotrophs, or decay bacteria, are important in the normal balance of a healthy aquarium, but only in moderation. Each stage in biological filtration depends on stable activity by the other stages. If the organic matter in the tank suddenly increases, the activity of the heterotrophs increases in proportion. This means that an excessive amount of ammonia is produced in a very short time—in many cases too short for the nitrifying bacteria to handle it. If the ammonia level suddenly increases, it may take up to three days for the nitrifiers to adjust to the higher level. This is more than sufficient time for your animals to die from ammonia poisoning.

In extreme cases the bacterial population reaches its maximum ability to convert the ammonia and any above this level will simply accumulate. The filter bed, don't forget, is limited in size and has only so many surfaces on the gravel to which bacteria can attach; it can, therefore, support only so many organisms.

Nitrifying bacteria need oxygen, just like the animals you are displaying. When the air to a subgravel filter is shut off, the nitrifying bacteria start to die. Other bacteria which do not require oxygen to live start decomposing the nitrifiers and elevating the overall level of decay. This releases even more ammonia.

In summary, biological filtration is the basic common denominator in marine aquarium keeping. Without its stabilizing influence on the chemistry of the water, few animals can survive for long.

3.3 MECHANICAL FILTRATION

Mechanical filtration is the removal of suspended particles from the water. It occurs mainly in the filter bed, augmented to some extent by the filter fiber in the outside filter. Without this process the water would be turbid instead of clear.

In the aquarium the filter bed doubles as a mechanical and biological filter, trapping minute particles as they drift to the bottom as well as providing attachment sites for beneficial bacteria. Both types of filtration are more effective if lots of surfaces are exposed to the water. For this reason rough, angular gravels are preferable to smooth, rounded types.

Gravels, of course, vary in grain size. These sizes are defined in Table 6. As stated earlier, gravel about $\frac{3}{16}$ in. (2–5 mm) makes ideal filter bed material. Sand is too fine, for it eventually packs down and impedes water flow through the bed. Coarse gravels have the opposite effect; they allow much of the particulate matter to pass completely through the bed.

Table 6   Definition of Grain Sizes

Designation		Size (in.)	Size (mm)
Gravel	Boulders	20 or greater	500 or greater
	Cobbles	1–20	25–500
	Pebbles	$\frac{7}{16}$–1	10–25
	Fine gravel	$\frac{1}{16}$–$\frac{7}{16}$	2–11
Sand	Very coarse sand		1–2
	Coarse sand		0.5–1.0
	Medium sand		0.250–0.500
	Fine sand		0.100–0.250
	Very fine sand		0.050–0.100

MECHANISMS OF PARTICLE REMOVAL

Straining. In straining, the particles are simply trapped against another surface. If the particle is larger than the space between gravel grains, it is strained out mechanically, like tea leaves in a tea strainer. Particles that are smaller than the average space are trapped somewhere along the way by chance contact. Straining is shown diagrammatically in Figure 23.

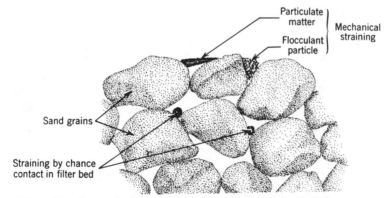

Figure 23   Removal of suspended particulate matter by straining.

Inertial Impaction or Sedimentation. Particles circulating in aquarium water have weight. As they move through the filter bed they do not always follow the *streamline*, or normal flow of the water, but settle by the force of gravity on the surface of a gravel grain, as in Figure 24.

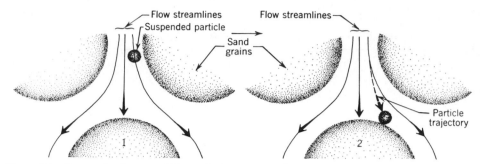

Figure 24   Removal of suspended particulate matter by inertial impaction or sedimentation.

Interception. Many particles do move in the streamline. They are removed when they come in contact with a gravel surface, as shown in the diagram in Figure 25.

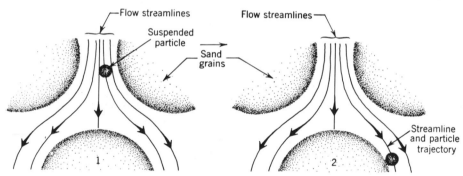

Figure 25   Removal of suspended particulate matter by interception.

Flocculation. Large particles overtake smaller particles, join them, and form still larger ones called flocculant particles. The process by which they are formed is *flocculation* and is shown diagrammatically in Figure 26.

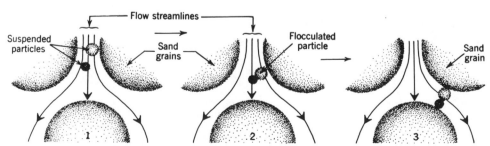

Figure 26   Removal of suspended particulate matter by flocculation.

Adhesion. Flocculant particles become attached to the surface of gravel grains as they pass by. Because of the force of the flowing water, some material is torn away before it can become firmly attached and is pushed deeper into the filter bed. As the bed becomes clogged, the force increases to a point at which no additional material can be removed. Now some of the material may break through the bottom of the filter, causing the sudden appearance of turbid, brown water sometimes seen spurting from the airlifts of old aquariums. Adhesion is shown diagrammatically in Figure 27.

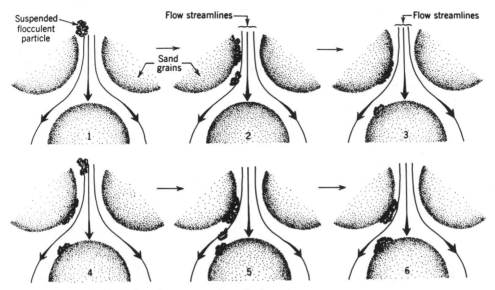

Figure 27   Removal of flocculant matter by adhesion.

3.4   CHEMICAL FILTRATION

Small volumes of pure sea water are colorless; larger volumes are tinged with blue. The metabolic activities of animals alter the color of the water. Although its clarity may remain unchanged, old water eventually assumes a greenish-yellow cast. This is caused by an increase in the amount of dissolved organic matter, which is mostly yellow in color. Only a part of this material is removed in the filter bed by the activity of heterotrophic bacteria. Mechanical filtration can remove particulate matter efficiently, but not substances in solution. Chemical filtration remains the only technique that can eliminate these dissolved organics.

Chemical filtration is defined as the removal of dissolved organics by adsorption, airstripping, or direct oxidation to simpler chemical substances. For adsorption, activated carbon is the most reliable means. Airstripping removes organics by foam fractionation, and both ozone and ultraviolet (UV) irradiation oxidize organic compounds into simpler constituents.

Besides imparting a sickly yellow color to the water, high levels of dissolved organics are undesirable because they increase the oxidative activities of heterotrophic bacteria, gradually lowering the pH of the water and using up an excessive amount of oxygen. In small filter beds with low turnover rates, the increased activity of heterotrophs sometimes causes a drop in pH below the minimum threshold (7.5) and reduces the oxygen to a point at which the animals become partially asphyxiated.

Many organics, especially those excreted directly into the water by the animals, may be mildly toxic. This is manifested by decreased reproductive capacity, general decrease in resistance to disease, and inhibition of growth. Only a few of these chemical compounds have so far been isolated, but research indicates they are more prevalent than formerly believed.

Dissolved organics are direct precursors of ammonia; that is, any organic material can be broken down to form a certain amount of ammonia and should be removed, if possible, before it can be mineralized.

In water chemistry the level of organics can be measured as TOC (*total organic carbon*). Unfortunately no test kit is available that measures the level of organics in water and no limits have been established for TOC thresholds in marine aquariums. This leaves the hobbyist guessing and taking preventive measures against something that can't really be defined. For the time being, however, there is no choice.

ACTIVATED CARBON

Activated carbon, or charcoal, is a porous substance containing up to 98% pure carbon. It is produced by heating carbonaceous materials like cellulose, wood, nut shells, and coal to between 900 and 1100 F (500–600 C) in the absence of air. The activation process takes place afterward when the material is heated again, this time in steam, to a temperature of 1650 F (900 C). Activation is accomplished when most of the hydrocarbons have been removed.

Adsorptive properties of an activated carbon are largely a function of the startling amount of internal surface area. One cubic inch (about $\frac{1}{2}$-oz) of an average activated carbon contains a total surface area of 25 million square inches. Figure 28 is a diagram of an activated carbon granule.

Under ideal conditions activated carbon can remove up to 50% of its own weight in dissolved organics. No other material can perform so efficiently at such low cost. This makes it cheaper to discard spent carbon rather than regenerate it. Regeneration, in fact, cannot be accomplished successfully except under steam pressure, an impractical technique for hobbyists.

No one knows how long activated carbon can remain adsorptive in the average aquarium. A good practice is to replace half every two weeks with new material. Remember to wash it first in tap water to remove the dust.

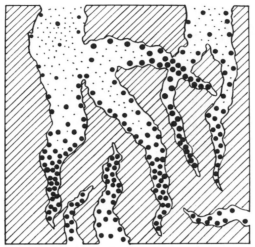

Figure 28   Diagrammatic   cross   section   of   an   activated   carbon   granule   showing   adsorbed organic molecules in the pores.

AIRSTRIPPING

Some organic compounds show reduced boundary tension between themselves and the water in which they are dissolved. Normally they are concentrated at the surface, although some are dispersed throughout the water. These compounds, which can be removed by disrupting the air-water interface with a strong curtain of air, are *surface active*.

The process used to remove surface-active compounds is known as *airstripping*, or protein skimming. Airstripping is the term used here. Essentially, a volume of water is restricted in a vertical column into which air is injected. As the air and the water mix, surface-active agents are removed from solution by foaming and the foam is collected in a dry chamber located above the water line. This chamber is emptied periodically. Two airstripping devices are shown in Figures 29 and 30.

In Figure 29 the device shown is *direct-current*, meaning that the water being treated and the air are moving in the same direction. Air from the compressor enters through the airstone (2). As it rises in the column (1) it mixes with the water. Coagulated surface-active agents build up as a frothy scum on the surface of the water in this chamber (3). When it has accumulated in sufficient quantity, the foam is forced through a connecting tube into the collection chamber above (5). Treated water is returned to the aquarium tank through a spout (4).

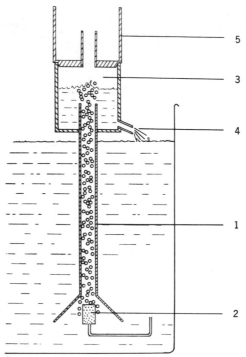

Figure 29   Direct-current airstripping device. Numbers are explained in the text.

A *counter-current* airstripper is shown in Figure 30. The water being treated moves downward against the rising stream of air. In this device air enters through the airstone (4) and rises in the contact tube (2). Aquarium water enters the contact tube near the top (3). The top of the contact tube also serves as a separation chamber. Separated surface-active agents pass into the collection chamber (1), which can be removed and cleaned. Treated water passes from a connecting tube (6) near the bottom of the contact tube and is airlifted back into the aquarium (5). Counter-current designs are more effective because the water is in contact with the air for a longer period of time.

The overall *chemical oxygen demand* (COD) level (the portion of the TOC that can be oxidized) is lowered by removing surface-active agents. Evidence exists that some nonsurface-active substances may also be removed, although little is known about them. Some suspended solids are taken out by a mechanism known as *froth flotation* in which particles become bound up in the foam. In this case airstripping augments mechanical filtration.

Many hobbyists are under the impression that airstripping removes a significant amount of ammonia from aquarium water. This isn't true. Experimental evidence has shown that 85% ammonia removal by airstripping does not take place until the pH of the water reaches 10.0, or far above the level that can be tolerated by most marine animals. Ninety-five percent of the ammonia is not removed until a pH of 11.5 is attained.

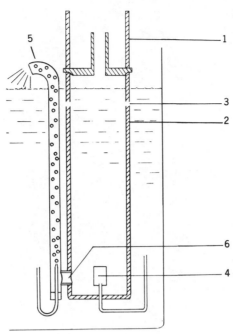

Figure 30   Counter-current airstripping device. Numbers are explained in the text.

OZONE

Ozone, or triatomic oxygen (O_3), has received much attention among hobbyists in recent years but mostly for the wrong reasons. Many have looked to ozone as a miracle cure for fish diseases, others as a means of directly oxidizing the ammonia in aquarium water. Both hopes have now been proved unfounded under controlled experimentation. A typical aquarium ozonator is shown in Figure 31.

As far as disease goes, ozone may prevent reinfection of a fish by microscopic organisms floating freely in the water. This is a useful function in closed-system aquariums in which the water is continuously recirculated. The fish, however, has not been "cured" in the true sense. It still retains those pathogens that adhere to the surface of its body, since to put sufficient ozone into the water to kill them would jeopardize the fish. Ozone is therefore more a prophylactic, or preventive, measure than a cure.

The highly unstable molecule, triatomic oxygen, is a powerful oxidizing agent capable of destroying bacteria, protozoans, and many organic compounds on contact. The term *oxidation*, as used in reference to ozone, means that when a molecule of ozone comes in contact with another compound demonstrating *oxygen demand* (when it can chemically accept an oxygen atom) it flies apart. The extra oxygen atom in the ozone reacts with the organic compound and "oxidizes" it, leaving a now-stable oxygen molecule (O_2) behind.

Six factors affect the efficiency of ozone.

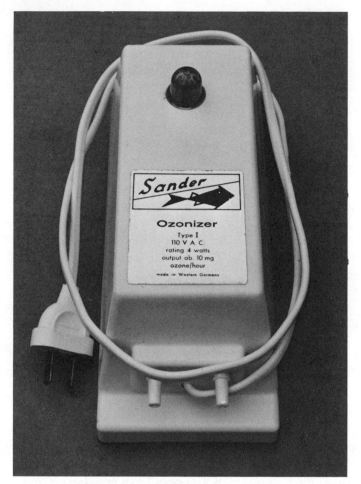

Figure 31   An ozonator.

Contact Time. The most important factor is the amount of time the aquarium water is in contact with the ozone. Many organics are oxidized slowly. In most aquarium setups ozone mixes with the water inside a contact tube, as in Figures 29 and 30. The purpose of the contact tube is to separate a small portion of the water into a restricted area in which it can react more effectively with the ozone.

Airstrippers can be used for ozonation. Simply disconnect the air compressor and substitute an ozonator. As in airstripping, counter-current designs work better than direct-current designs because contact time is increased.

The *half-life* of ozone in water, or the amount of time necessary for half of it to dissipate, is about 20 minutes. In waters with a high organic load the contact time required to reduce the dissolved COD level from 40 to 15 ppm is an hour. A level of 15 ppm is about normal for a marine aquarium. (As with TOC, there is no way of quickly measuring the COD level).

Organics in the Water. The nature of the organic substances in the water, and also their amount, largely determines the quantity oxidized. An initially high organic level results in a higher percentage of material oxidized, provided contact time is adequate. The remaining compounds are removed more slowly because they are less susceptible to oxidation by ozone. A curve illustrating the oxidation process would at first show high rates of removal followed by a gradual tapering off.

Prefiltration. Filtration of the water before it reaches the contact tube increases the efficiency of ozonation. Biological filtration (specifically, heterotrophic activity) removes compounds that would hardly be oxidized by ozone. This is particularly evident when TOC is used as an index. Biological filtration lowers the TOC level, which in turn results in less TOC in the effluent water leaving the ozone contact tube.

pH. The optimum pH range for effective oxidation of organics by ozone is 6.6 to 8.3. Since this is within the normal range of marine aquarium water, nothing more need be said about it.

Temperature. Ozone becomes more unstable with increasing temperature. At higher temperatures more is dissipated before it performs any oxidation, and the result is reduced efficiency. The animals in an aquarium are acclimated to certain temperatures, and these should not be changed to make ozonation more efficient. Reduced effectiveness in ozonation is much less risky than stressing the animals by suddenly lowering their water temperature.

Air or Oxygen. Ozone generation can be doubled by substituting oxygen for air at the ozonator intake.

ULTRAVIOLET IRRADIATION

Cursory experiments with freshwater fishes indicate that when ultraviolet (UV) irradiation is properly used the numbers of free-floating viruses and bacteria are decreased. Control of protozoans requires substantially higher dosage levels and current data are inconclusive on this score. Viruses and bacteria are also killed by UV in sea water, and certain stages in the life histories of pathogenic protozoans are probably affected too, but no definite proof exists.

The major benefit of using UV irradiation is the control of unattached microbes. This lowers the incidence of infection on a group of fishes within the close confines of an aquarium, in which diseases are easily transferred from one to another. It is possible that continuous use of UV lowers the level of dissolved organics to some extent, but this is speculative. A UV sterilizer and its parts are shown in Figure 32.

Ultraviolet dosage is measured in microwatt seconds per square centimeter (μWs/cm^2). Any useful UV device should be designed to deliver a minimum of 35,000 μWs/cm^2 to the water being treated. To meet this re-

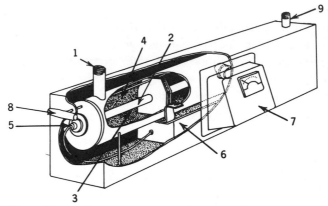

Figure 32   A UV sterilizer and component parts: (1) *inlet;* (2) *UV lamp;* (3) *jacket;* (4) *purification chamber;* (5) *lamp socket;* (6) *ballast for quick starts;* (7) *UV intensity meter;* (8) *hand wiper;* (9) *outlet.*

quirement a simple rule of thumb may be applied. *The flow rate should be no greater than 0.2 gallon per minute (gpm) per effective inch of ultraviolet lamp (intensity), and the contact time within the purification chamber should not be less than 15 seconds.* These figures are based on a UV lamp with an output of 120 μW/cm^2 at a distance of 1 m. If lamps with lower output are employed, an adjustment in the formula must be made; for example, if the formula indicates that 30 inches of lamp are required and a lamp with an output of 60 μW is used, then 60 inches of this type of lamp would be necessary, since the output is half the standard 120 μWs/cm^2 lamp.

Intensity. As seen from the rule above, dosage is partly a function of intensity. As used here, "intensity" is actually the number of lamps, since the answer derived from any calculation must then be converted into commercial lamps of standard lengths. This becomes clear in the example below.

Suppose that in a large aquarium the turnover rate (T) = 12 gpm, intensity (I) = 0.2 gpm per inch of lamp, and N = number of inches of lamp needed to sterilize the water.

$$N = \frac{T}{I} = \frac{12}{0.2} = 60 \text{ inches of lamp.}$$

If 30-in. lamps are used, two of them would be necessary.

Volume of the Contact Chamber. The other aspect of dosage, the volume of the contact chamber, is determined by the contact time and flow rate. Contact time must be a minimum of 15 seconds, or one-fourth of a minute. Therefore the *volume of the contact chamber (in gallons) equals the turnover rate divided by four.* Using the figures from the first example, if the turnover rate equals 12 gpm, then 12 ÷ 4 = 3 gal.

Let's take another example, but this time with some variations. The length of the lamp is known to be 12 in. (Length of the lamp, incidently, is *effective length*, meaning the bulb only—don't include the sockets at each end of the unit). Its output is $55\mu W/cm^2$ at 1 m. We also know that the turnover rate through the unit will be 2.4 gpm. We have to find the number of lamps needed and also the required volume of the contact chamber.

Because the output of the lamp is only about half what is required ($55 \mu W/cm^2$ at 1 m instead of 120), the intensity must also be decreased by half (from 0.2 gpm per inch of lamp to 0.1). Therefore, the intensity equals $12 \times 0.1 = 1.2$ gpm per inch of lamp.

$$N = \frac{T}{I} = \frac{2.4}{1.2} = 2 \text{ lamps, each 12 in. long.}$$

$$V = \frac{T}{4} = \frac{2.4}{4} = 0.6 \text{ gal.}$$

Technical data for some typical UV lamps are given in Table 7. Intensity and chamber volume can be determined from the figures given there, as long as the turnover rate of the water is known.

Table 7   Technical Data for Some Typical Ultraviolet Lamps

Effective Length (in.)	Watts	Ultraviolet Output ($\mu W/cm^2$ at 1 m)	UV lamp (gpm/in.)	Rating per Lamp (gpm)
11	20	28	0.05	0.55
20	14	35	0.06	1.20
30	29	73	0.12	3.60
10	16	55	0.09	0.90
30	39	120	0.20	6.00
60	65	120	0.20	12.00

Basically, there are three factors affecting the efficiency of UV irradiation.

Contact Time. The efficiency of any UV lamp is increased by prolonging its exposure to a given volume of water. A minimum of 15 sec is recommended.

Prefiltration. Filtering the water before passing it through a UV unit increases the effectiveness of the irradiation process.

Design. The design of a good UV unit incorporates an air space around the bulb, separating it from the contact chamber (Figure 32). This air space keeps the bulb from becoming coated with the organics in the water that would impair its efficiency. It also makes it possible to change a bulb without disassembling the unit.

Part of the energy produced by a UV lamp is heat, and the air space will be approximately 50 F higher than the water temperature. This increases the efficiency of the unit without significantly increasing the temperature of the water.

The inner cylinder, or "jacket," which surrounds the bulb and separates it from the water being sterilized, should be made of quartz to assure maximum transmittance. The walls of the contact chamber must be glass or stainless steel. Plastics are unsuitable, since all of them—PVC included—are destroyed by UV irradiation.

An ultraviolet lamp does not "burn out," and there is no other visual means of determining loss of efficiency; that is, the bulb does not dim or flicker with prolonged use. Ultraviolet irradiation is produced when the mercury contained within the lamp vaporizes. Some of this mercury gradually coats the inside of the glass, filtering out an increasingly greater percentage of the rays being generated. When the output declines by 25%, the *effective life* of the unit has been reached. In aquarium applications this is about a year if the equipment has been used continuously.

3.5 EVALUATION OF METHODS

Biological filtration is unquestionably the most important of the three types of filtration, and a subgravel filter has no adequate substitute.

Mechanical filtration is accomplished by gravel in the filter bed, augmented to a certain extent by the filter fiber. The combination should be sufficient to prevent even minor turbidity problems.

Before starting an evaluation of the different methods of chemical filtration one general rule can be set forth: never use chemical filtration on any aquarium undergoing treatment with antibiotics or chemotheraputics. By and large, these are organic compounds and chemical filtration removes them.

Activated carbon is recommended for all marine aquariums, regardless of their size. No harmful effects from this material have been reported, and on the positive side it is known to adsorb dissolved organics continuously and in considerable quantity. In most small aquariums in which the animal loading is within normal limitations, no other means of chemical filtration is necessary.

Airstripping supplements mechanical filtration to a limited extent by froth flotation, but it is generally insignificant. Activated carbon undoubtedly takes up a portion of the surface-active agents present in the water. This becomes obvious when activated carbon and an airstripper are used on the same aquarium. Eventually the airstripper stops producing foam, which indicates that the activated carbon has lowered the level of surface-active agents below 1 ppm (the minimum level for froth formation to occur). Airstrippers are optional equipment and usually aren't necessary.

Treatment with ozone and irradiation with ultraviolet should be used only on an interim basis, such as during an outbreak of disease. Running an ozonator or UV unit continuously serves no purpose. If the animals are carefully fed and are not overcrowded, free-floating bacteria and protozoans will not be a problem. Maintaining a healthy environment is a far better prophylactic than ozone treatment or UV irradiation could ever be.

Ultraviolet irradiation is preferable to ozone. Ozone has two major drawbacks in the aquarium. First, it is difficult to regulate the amount entering the water. This is due partly to the unstable nature of the ozone molecule and partly to the inexact design of available ozonators. Second, there is no convenient test for measuring the amount of ozone present in the water, and overdosing is an ever-present danger. Such is not the case with UV, in which the lethal agent is enclosed in a jacket. The rays never come into direct contact with the animals, and since UV irradiation is not a chemical process there is no danger of using too much.

Chapter Four

≋≋≋≋≋≋

Thinking Wet

4.1 THE REASON

Marine fishes and invertebrates are in intimate contact with their environment. Their gills are exposed to the water around them and in many cases even their outermost skins are composed of living tissue. For our purposes they might be considered as physiological extensions of the water in which they live.

The opposite is true of land animals, ourselves included. Our dead skins act as impervious shields for the delicate life processes ticking away inside. It matters little if we are wet or dry, warm or cold; within reasonable limits, our bodily functions go on working as if the environment outside did not exist at all.

The marine aquarist, being a land creature, must be conscious of environmental factors in the water that might affect his aquatic animals. He must learn to "think wet."

4.2 AMMONIA

In Chapter 3 we noted that any uneaten food or dead animals left rotting in the tank will cause an increase in the ammonia level. Ammonia, it was explained, is toxic, but no mention was made of how toxic it really is.

A few years ago a research biologist in the state of Washington discovered that un-ionized ammonia (NH_3) in the concentration of only 0.006 ppm (six parts ammonia in one billion parts water) caused gill deformities in young salmon. Others have confirmed that a level of 0.1 ppm un-ionized ammonia (one part ammonia to 10 million parts water) is usually lethal to the more delicate fishes and invertebrates.

There is also a case on record in which fishes in a research laboratory were killed by ammonia emanating from a white rat colony in the next room. This indicates that airborne ammonia is highly soluble, and no cleaning with household ammonia or commercial window cleaners should be done in the vicinity of an aquarium.

If you think this leaves little margin for error, you are absolutely right. No aquarist, regardless of his skill, can maintain an aquarium successfully when it has a chronic ammonia problem.

4.3 OXYGENATION

Early aquarists thought that bubbles from artificial aeration totally dissolved as they rose in the water column, thus providing enough oxygen for the animals to live. We now know that such bubbling is mainly a technique for moving bottom water to the surface and that most oxygenation occurs at the *air-water interface* (the surface of the water exposed to the atmosphere).

Air holds much more oxygen than water. In nature the wind, tides, currents, and spin of the earth keep water in motion, continuously raising underlying layers to the surface and oxygenating them. This activity must be artificially simulated in the aquarium. Airlifts are the means for doing it.

Water from underneath the subgravel filter is lifted to the top of the aquarium and spilled across the surface, as shown in Figure 16. The surface is agitated in the process, and gaseous oxygen from the atmosphere enters the aquarium at the air-water interface by simple diffusion. Without the agitation provided by the airlifts aerobic bacteria and the animals would soon combine to deplete the available oxygen and eventually asphyxiate themselves.

4.4 pH

The pH is a measure of the acidity or alkalinity of the water, read in units on a scale of 0 to 14. A pH of exactly 7 is neutral. From 0 to 7 is considered acidic, from 7 to 14 alkaline.

The pH of the open sea is close to 8.3, or somewhat alkaline. Marine animals need an alkaline pH, ideally within the range of 7.5 to 8.3. Many aquarists believe that pH is the most important factor in keeping an aquarium but actually it is not so critical as salt content, ammonia, dissolved oxygen, or temperature.

The calcareous gravel in the filter bed maintains a stable pH for the life of the aquarium. Two ions affecting pH are *bicarbonate* (HCO_3^-) and *carbonate* (CO_3^{2-}). As long as they are being released into the water, the pH will stay above neutral. In fact, if the tank isn't overcrowded, the gravel will keep the pH within required limits without your doing a thing.

Calcareous gravel contains a high percentage of calcium carbonate, which slowly dissolves and separates into calcium ions (Ca^{2+}) and carbonate ions. As seen from the following equation, when the reaction shifts to the right (top arrows), carbonate ions are released and the result is a high pH. As it shifts to the left (bottom arrows), carbonate combines with other elements, making it unavailable in solution. This lowers the pH.

$$2H_2O + 2CO_2 \rightleftharpoons 2H_2CO_3 \rightleftharpoons H^+ + 2HCO_3^- \rightleftharpoons 2H^+ + 2CO_3^{2-}.$$

4.5   TEMPERATURE

A fish or invertebrate is a cold-blooded animal with a body temperature essentially the same as the temperature of the water surrounding it. If the water is too cold, the animal's metabolism is slowed down and it has difficulty carrying out normal life processes. If the water is too warm, metabolism accelerates to such a degree that the animal "burns itself out." If the temperature fluctuates, the metabolism of the animal oscillates back and forth in an effort to keep up. This last situation, needless to say, is as unhealthy as the first two.

Temperature also affects the quantity of dissolved oxygen in solution. At higher elevations the oxygen level will be less, as shown in Table 9 on page 59; for example, at a temperature of 50 F (10 C) there are 9 ppm dissolved oxygen, whereas at 72 F (22 C), there are only 7.1 ppm.

The temperature of an aquarium must be kept constant. If it varies even a degree or two, another stress factor is added to plague the animals. The ideal temperature range for a tropical aquarium was given in Chapter 2 as 70 to 73 F (21–23 C). The term "range" here does not imply that the temperature can fluctuate. It means choose a value somewhere in between and keep it stable.

4.6   SALT CONTENT

Osmoregulation describes the ability of animals to control the amounts of salt and water in their tissues. As a rule, marine creatures have slightly lower salt levels than sea water. This type of osmoregulation is termed *hypoosmoregulation* ("hypo" meaning less than). Freshwater animals, on the other hand, maintain salt in their bodies at greater concentrations than the water in which they live.

Even though they are bathed in a watery solution, marine animals must drink sea water constantly or die of dehydration. The sea, being a saltier medium, draws water from the tissues. To offset this mechanism fishes consume water at a rate of 0.2 to 0.5% of their body weight per hour. To conserve further body water fishes produce very little urine. The excess salts in the water they drink are excreted through the mucus cells in the skin, in the feces, by the kidneys, and especially by certain cells in the gills.

Marine animals are easily stressed when the salt content of the water is suddenly thrown out of balance. For this reason the specific gravity of your sea water should vary as little as possible. The acceptable limits of variation are given in Chapter 5, Section 7.

Chapter Five

Testing and Troubleshooting

5.1 THE PURPOSE

Checking the chemistry of the sea water is critical to successful marine aquarium keeping because water quality determines whether the life-support processes in the filter bed are continuing at steady and reasonable rates. This type of quality control is mandatory for the serious hobbyist.

All the tests described in this chapter should be conducted weekly and the results recorded on a data sheet similar to the one shown in Figure 33. This provides a continuing history on each aquarium and enables you to correlate outbreaks of disease with changes in water quality. On the positive side it will enable you to reproduce certain water conditions in case your animals spawn or do exceptionally well.

The troubleshooting keys give specific courses of action to take when water quality factors fall below acceptable limits.

Tank _____   Month _____   Year _____

Date				
Ammonia N				
Total ammonia				
% un–ionized				
Nitrite N				
Nitrite ion				
Nitrate N				
Nitrate ion				
Temperature				
pH				
Specific gravity				
Dissolved O_2				

Conversion factors
Ammonia N x 1.3 = total ammonia.
Nitrite N x 3.3 = nitrite ion.
Nitrate N x 4.4 = nitrate ion.

Figure 33   Data sheet for aquarium water chemistry.

5.2 AMMONIA

ACCEPTABLE RANGE

Less than 0.01 ppm un-ionized ammonia (NH_3).

TESTING

The ammonia reading you get with any colorimetric test kit is the total ammonia, and until converted to parts per million of un-ionized ammonia it is a meaningless value. Ionized ammonia (NH_4^+) and un-ionized ammonia (NH_3) are both present in water, but the ionized form is not taken up by aquatic animals, since it cannot cross tissue barriers.

It is important to visualize un-ionized ammonia simply as a part of the total ammonia with a concentration that varies with the temperature and pH of the water. The proportion of un-ionized ammonia increases with a rise in these two factors. As shown in Table 8, the un-ionized ammonia in solution at 72 F (22 C) and a pH of 8.3 is 8.31%, whereas at the same temperature but a lower pH value (7.7) it is only 2.23%. This significant difference proves that from the standpoint of ammonia a high pH is not favorable.

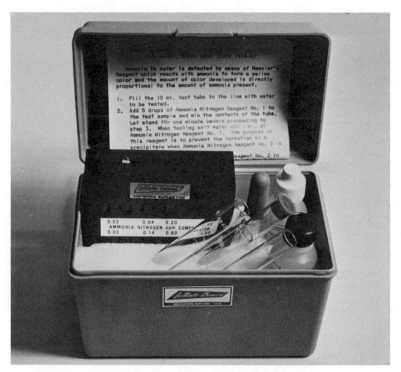

Figure 34   A kit for measuring ammonia N in sea water.

Most test kits currently available, such as the one in Figure 34, do not measure ionized or un-ionized ammonia directly but give a value for ammonia nitrogen (ammonia N) instead. It simply means that you are determining the N in NH_4^+. This is perfectly acceptable, provided the figure derived is multiplied by 1.3 to obtain total NH_4^+.

HOW TO DETERMINE PPM UN-IONIZED AMMONIA

1. Measure the ammonia N according to instructions with the test kit.
2. Multiply the value obtained by 1.3.
3. Determine the temperature and pH of the water.
4. Turn to Table 8 and locate the value corresponding to the temperature and pH of your water.
5. Convert this value to a decimal fraction by moving the decimal point two places to the left (e.g., 25.30 becomes 0.2530).
6. Multiply this number by the reading for total NH_4^+ (Step 2). This gives you the quantity of un-ionized ammonia in ppm.

Table 8   Percentage of Un-ionized Ammonia in Aqueous

pH	Centigrade 5 Fahrenheit 41.0	6 42.8	7 44.6	8 46.4	9 48.2	10 50.0	11 51.8	12 53.6	13 55.4	14 57.2
6.5	0.04	0.04	0.05	0.05	0.06	0.06	0.06	0.07	0.07	0.08
6.6	0.05	0.05	0.06	0.06	0.07	0.07	0.08	0.09	0.09	0.10
6.7	0.06	0.07	0.07	0.08	0.09	0.09	0.10	0.11	0.12	0.13
6.8	0.08	0.09	0.09	0.10	0.11	0.12	0.13	0.14	0.15	0.16
6.9	0.10	0.11	0.12	0.13	0.14	0.15	0.16	0.17	0.19	0.20
7.0	0.12	0.14	0.15	0.16	0.17	0.19	0.20	0.21	0.24	0.25
7.1	0.16	0.17	0.19	0.20	0.22	0.23	0.26	0.27	0.30	0.32
7.2	0.20	0.22	0.23	0.25	0.27	0.29	0.32	0.34	0.37	0.40
7.3	0.25	0.27	0.30	0.32	0.34	0.37	0.40	0.43	0.47	0.51
7.4	0.31	0.34	0.37	0.40	0.43	0.47	0.51	0.54	0.59	0.64
7.5	0.39	0.43	0.47	0.50	0.54	0.59	0.64	0.68	0.74	0.80
7.6	0.49	0.54	0.59	0.63	0.68	0.74	0.80	0.85	0.93	1.00
7.7	0.62	0.68	0.74	0.80	0.86	0.92	1.01	1.07	1.17	1.26
7.8	0.78	0.85	0.93	1.00	1.08	1.16	1.27	1.35	1.46	1.58
7.9	0.98	1.07	1.16	1.25	1.35	1.46	1.59	1.69	1.83	1.98
8.0	1.22	1.34	1.46	1.58	1.70	1.83	1.10	2.12	2.30	2.48
8.1	1.54	1.68	1.83	1.98	2.13	2.29	2.50	2.65	2.88	3.11
8.2	1.93	2.11	2.29	2.48	2.67	2.86	3.12	3.32	3.59	3.88
8.3	2.41	2.64	2.87	3.10	3.33	3.58	3.90	4.14	4.48	4.84
8.4	3.02	3.30	3.59	3.87	4.16	4.46	4.87	5.15	5.58	6.01
8.5	3.77	4.12	4.47	4.82	5.18	5.55	6.05	6.40	6.92	7.45
8.6	4.70	5.13	5.57	5.99	6.44	6.89	7.50	7.93	8.56	9.21
8.7	5.85	6.38	6.91	7.43	7.97	8.53	9.26	9.78	10.54	11.32
8.8	7.25	7.90	8.54	9.18	9.84	10.50	11.38	12.01	12.92	13.84
8.9	8.96	9.74	10.52	11.28	12.07	12.87	13.92	14.66	15.74	16.82
9.0	11.02	11.96	12.89	13.80	14.74	15.88	16.91	17.78	19.04	20.30

Ammonia Solutions at Different pH and Temperature Values

15	16	17	18	19	20	21	22	23	24	25
59.0	60.8	62.6	64.4	66.2	68.0	69.8	71.0	73.4	75.2	77.0
0.09	0.09	0.10	0.10	0.12	0.13	0.13	0.14	0.16	0.17	0.18
0.10	0.12	0.13	0.13	0.15	0.16	0.17	0.18	0.20	0.21	0.22
0.14	0.15	0.16	0.17	0.18	0.20	0.21	0.23	0.25	0.26	0.28
0.17	0.19	0.20	0.21	0.23	0.25	0.27	0.29	0.31	0.33	0.35
0.22	0.23	0.25	0.27	0.29	0.32	0.34	0.36	0.39	0.42	0.44
0.27	0.29	0.31	0.34	0.37	0.40	0.42	0.45	0.49	0.52	0.55
0.34	0.37	0.39	0.42	0.46	0.50	0.53	0.57	0.62	0.66	0.70
0.43	0.46	0.50	0.53	0.58	0.63	0.67	0.71	0.77	0.83	0.88
0.54	0.58	0.62	0.67	0.73	0.79	0.84	0.90	0.97	1.04	1.10
0.68	0.73	0.78	0.84	0.91	0.99	1.05	1.13	1.22	1.30	1.38
0.85	0.92	0.98	1.06	1.15	1.24	1.32	1.42	1.53	1.63	1.73
1.07	1.16	1.24	1.33	1.44	1.56	1.66	1.78	1.92	2.05	2.17
1.35	1.45	1.55	1.67	1.81	1.96	2.08	2.23	2.41	2.57	2.72
1.69	1.82	1.95	2.09	2.26	2.45	2.61	2.79	3.01	3.21	3.39
2.12	2.29	2.44	2.62	2.83	3.06	3.26	3.48	3.76	4.01	4.24
2.65	2.86	3.05	3.28	3.54	3.83	4.07	4.35	4.69	4.99	5.28
3.32	3.58	3.81	4.09	4.42	4.77	5.07	5.41	5.83	6.21	6.55
4.14	4.46	4.75	5.10	5.50	5.94	6.30	6.72	7.23	7.69	8.11
5.16	5.55	5.90	6.33	6.82	7.36	7.80	8.31	8.94	9.49	10.00
6.41	6.89	7.32	7.84	8.44	9.09	9.62	10.24	10.99	11.66	12.27
7.98	8.52	9.04	9.68	10.40	11.18	11.82	12.56	13.45	14.25	14.97
9.79	10.49	11.12	11.88	12.74	13.68	14.44	15.31	16.37	17.30	18.14
12.02	12.86	13.61	14.51	15.53	16.63	17.53	18.54	19.77	20.84	21.82
14.68	15.67	16.55	17.61	18.30	20.07	21.11	22.27	23.68	24.90	26.00
17.80	18.96	19.98	21.20	22.57	24.02	25.19	26.51	28.09	29.44	30.66
21.42	22.75	23.91	25.30	26.85	28.47	29.78	31.23	32.96	34.44	35.76

EXAMPLE.   Measured ammonia N = 0.30 ppm.
Temperature = 70 F (21 C).
pH = 7.9.
Percentage un-ionized ammonia (Table 8) = 3.26.

Therefore

$$0.30 \times 1.3 = 0.39.$$
$$0.39 \times 0.0326 = 0.012714.$$

Rounded off, this equals 0.013 ppm un-ionized ammonia.

If this had been an actual reading, it would have been above acceptable standards and some action to lower it would have been necessary. When you find too much ammonia in your aquarium, there are theoretically three areas of attack: lower the temperature, lower the pH, or lower the ammonia. The first two are impractical, unless these factors are also outside normal limits. (They were not in the above example). So the alternative is to find a way of lowering the total ammonia level. This can be done with the help of a troubleshooting key.

Here is how you use this key and all the others as well. Start with *A*. If you see, for example, that no uneaten food or dead animals have been left in the system for 12 hours or longer, go to *B*. If, however, uneaten food or dead animals are present, go to *AA* instead. Follow the key step by step in this manner until proper action has been taken and the problem solved.

TROUBLESHOOTING KEY FOR EXCESS AMMONIA

A   No uneaten food or dead animals left in the system
for 12 hours or longer . . . . *B*

AA   Uneaten food or dead animals left in the system.

Un-ionized ammonia level should be reduced to less than 0.01 ppm within two days after removal of the material. If not, change 25% of the water daily until the level stabilizes at less than 0.01 ppm. Measure for two days. Repeat this step if necessary.

B   No recent change in the animal population . . . . *C*

BB   More specimens recently added.

Measure the ammonia for three days until it stabilizes. If it does not, remove some of the animals and continue checking until the level remains within normal limits.

C   No organic contamination suspected . . . . *D*

CC   Organic contamination suspected (e.g., antibiotics, paint fumes, insecticides).

Replace the activated carbon, increase airstripping (if present) to maximum level, and change 50% of the water. If the ammonia still does not stabilize within five days, replace the activated carbon and change 10% of the water daily for three days.

D   No heavy metal poisoning suspected   .   .   .   . E
DD   System recently treated with a heavy metal.

Change 50% of the water and check the ammonia daily for three days. Repeat this step if necessary.

E   No recent increase in food input .   .   .   . F
EE   Food recently increased.

Ammonia stabilizes by itself within three days. If it does not, remove some of the animals and measure the ammonia for another three days. After the level stabilizes, return the animals to the aquarium one at a time, allowing two days between each.

F   Filter bed not recently cleaned   .   .   .   . G
FF   Filter recently cleaned and large amounts of detritus removed.

Ammonia stabilizes by itself within three days. If it does not, reduce the animal population and measure daily for three days. When the level stabilizes, return the animals to the tank one at a time, allowing two days between each.

G   Recent and significant change in specific gravity.
If the magnitude of the change is less than ±0.002, measure the ammonia for three days until it stabilizes. If the magnitude is greater than ±0.002, gradually adjust the specific gravity to its corrected value (see Section 7). Measure the ammonia level until it stabilizes at less than 0.01 ppm NH_3.

5.3   NITRITE

ACCEPTABLE RANGE

Less than 0.1 ppm as nitrite ion (NO_2^-).

TESTING

Nitrite has proved to be only slightly toxic to marine animals, though admittedly just a few have been tested so far. The purpose of measuring nitrite ion is not so much to monitor its potentially toxic levels (as in testing for ammonia) but rather to spot-check the progress of nitrification. Nitrite, of course, is the intermediate product between ammonia and nitrate. A low threshold level of less than 0.1 ppm is proof that nitrification is proceeding vigorously. A chronically high nitrite level indicates failure by nitrifying bacteria to convert it to nitrate.

The test kits normally available for testing nitrite measure nitrite N instead of nitrite ion (NO_2^-), and the value obtained must therefore be multiplied by a conversion factor.

HOW TO DETERMINE PPM NITRITE ION

1. Measure the nitrite N according to instructions with the test kit.
2. Multiply the value obtained by 3.3. This gives the quantity of NO_2^- present in ppm.

TROUBLESHOOTING KEY FOR EXCESS NITRITE

A   Subgravel filter has been operating for at least two weeks   . . . *B*

AA   Subgravel filter has been in operation for less than two weeks.

    Allow time for the filter bed to become conditioned. If after three weeks the nitrite level is still chronically high, proceed to B.

B   Animal load is well within estimated carrying capacity   . . . . *C*

BB   There are too many animals in the aquarium.

    Test the ammonia. If it is also high, remove some of the animals. Wait three days and check the ammonia and nitrite levels again.

C   No organic contamination suspected (e.g., antibiotics, paint fumes, insecticides)   . . . . *D*

CC   Organic contamination suspected.

    Replace the activated carbon, increase the turnover rate, and change 50% of the water. If the nitrite level does not stabilize after five days, again replace the activated carbon and change 25% of the water daily for another five days.

D   Aquarium recently treated with a heavy metal.

    Change 50% of the water and check the nitrite level daily for three days. Repeat this step until it stabilizes.

5.4   NITRATE

ACCEPTABLE RANGE

Less than 20.0 ppm as nitrate ion (NO_3^-).

TESTING

Nitrate is quite a bit less toxic than nitrite. In some of the older public aquariums, before the functions of biological filtration were well understood, nitrate ion sometimes reached such high levels that it was considered a major constituent of the sea water. Nevertheless it is never a good practice to allow the nitrate level to get out of hand. In a healthy, functioning filter bed the level should seldom exceed 20.0 ppm.

The formation of nitrate, as shown diagrammatically in Figure 21, is the last stage in nitrification. Afterward, denitrification takes over and reduces the nitrate to nitrous oxide or free nitrogen. If conditions are favorable, denitrification is adequate to keep the level within acceptable standards, although regular partial water changes are also helpful.

Kits available for testing nitrate usually measure nitrate N instead of the ion (NO_3^-), again making a simple mathematical conversion necessary.

HOW TO DETERMINE PPM NITRATE ION

1. Measure nitrate N according to instructions with the test kit.
2. Multiply the result by 4.4 to obtain ppm NO_3^-.

5.5   DISSOLVED OXYGEN

ACCEPTABLE RANGE

Not less than 1.0 ppm below saturation at any given temperature, with 5.0 ppm being the absolute lowest limit.

TESTING

The dissolved oxygen test kit (Figure 35) is perhaps the most difficult to use. Great care must be taken to make sure that the results are accurate. As shown in Table 9, dissolved oxygen and temperature are inversely proportional;

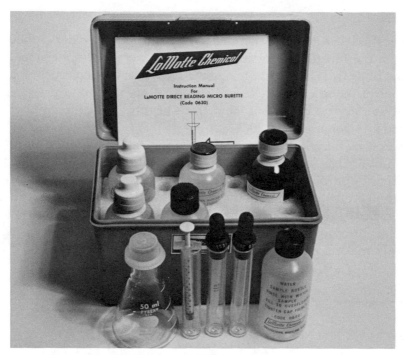

Figure 35   A kit for measuring dissolved oxygen in sea water.

that is, as one increases, the other decreases. The values in the table are at saturation. Under normal aquarium conditions readings near saturation should be expected. A low dissolved oxygen level is more dangerous at higher temperatures where no cushion is available to fall back on. According to the table, temperatures in the higher ranges are closer to the absolute minimum of 5.0 ppm, and warm-water aquariums are more likely to suffer from oxygen depletion than cold-water ones. This is not to say that all marine animals do better at low temperatures. Quite the contrary. It simply means that trouble with insufficient oxygen is more likely to occur when the water is warm and closer to the minimum limit allowed (5.0 ppm).

The animals in your aquarium use much of the oxygen, but don't forget the considerable needs of the bacteria. Aerobic bacteria require oxygen for their metabolic processes. In instances in which uneaten food or dead animals are left for a period of time, the heterotrophic activity sometimes increases,

Table 9   Dissolved Oxygen in Sea Water at
Different Temperatures

Temperature (F)	Temperature (C)	O₂ (ppm)
86	30	6.2
84	29	6.3
82	28	6.4
81	27	6.5
79	26	6.6
77	25	6.8
75	24	6.9
73	23	7.0
72	22	7.1
70	21	7.2
68	20	7.4
66	19	7.5
64	18	7.6
63	17	7.8
61	16	7.9
59	15	8.1
57	14	8.3
55	13	8.4
54	12	8.6
52	11	8.8
50	10	9.0
48	9	9.2
46	8	9.4
45	7	9.6
43	6	9.9
41	5	10.1
39	4	10.3
37	3	10.6
36	2	10.9
34	1	11.1

and decay is oxygen-consuming. Nitrifiers in the filter bed also utilize considerable amounts of oxygen. Ammonification, nitrification, and denitrification may be the cause—rather than the animals themselves—when low dissolved oxygen readings are obtained.

TROUBLESHOOTING KEY FOR INSUFFICIENT OXYGEN

A   Turnover rate acceptable . . . . *B*

AA   Turnover rate is low.

Increase turnover (add an additional air compressor if necessary). Test the dissolved oxygen level after two hours.

B   Surface agitation is inadequate.

Adjust the water level so that sufficient splashing action is obtained from the airlifts. Add an airstone if needed. Test the dissolved oxygen level after two hours.

5.6 *pH*

ACCEPTABLE RANGE

The acceptable pH range is 7.5 to 8.3.

TESTING

The measurement of pH is a simple exercise, although interpretation of the results is often confusing. The pH of water is an indicator of chemical changes that are taking place and should not be considered a significant factor by itself; for example, the bulk of the changes in water chemistry caused by bacteria are oxidative, which gradually lowers the pH. If the pH level should decline below the minimum standard, it might indicate excessive bacterial activity and steps would have to be taken to remedy it.

In freshwater aquariums the reaction given on page 47 sometimes shifts too far to the left. Under acidic conditions a very low pH reading would indicate the possibility of fish kills from carbon dioxide poisoning. Such an accident would be unlikely in marine aquariums, in which the high buffering capacity of sea water easily keeps the level at 7.5 or greater.

If the pH is low and animals are dying, look for whatever could cause a drop in pH.

TROUBLESHOOTING KEY FOR LOW PH

A   Filter gravel is composed entirely of calcareous material . . . . B
AA   Filter gravel not all calcareous.

Replace all gravel with conditioned dolomite, crushed oyster shell, crushed coral rock, or limestone. Test the pH every three days until it stabilizes.

B   Filter bed is at least 3 in. deep C
BB   Filter bed is less than 3 in. deep.

Add freshly washed calcareous gravel until the filter bed is at least 3 in. deep. Test the pH every three days until it stabilizes.

C   Dissolved organic level within reasonable limits . . . . D
CC   The water is greenish-yellow. Excessive organics suspected.

Replace 25% of the water with unused sea water. Replace half the activated carbon in the outside filter. Test the pH daily until the level stabilizes.

D Tank not overcrowded . . . . E

DD Tank definitely overcrowded. The recommended carrying capacity has been exceeded (three inches of animal per square foot of filter bed surface area).

Remove superfluous animals. Replace half the activated carbon in the outside filter. Check the pH level daily until it stabilizes.

E Detritus accumulation is heavy.

Siphon out the excess detritus. Replace half the activated carbon in the outside filter. Wash or replace the filter fiber.

5.7 SPECIFIC GRAVITY

ACCEPTABLE RANGE

At a given temperature, variation should not be greater than ±0.002 from the proper value, as given in Table 10.

TESTING

Everyone knows that cold air is heavier than warm air. The cool air in a room tends to sink to the floor, whereas the warm air rises. Water acts in the same manner. To say it another way, as the temperature decreases, water becomes denser. This phenomenon necessitates a simultaneous temperature reading whenever the specific gravity is measured; for instance, normal strength sea water has a specific gravity of 1.024 at 70 F (21 C). When cooled to 55 F (13 C), however, its specific gravity increases to 1.026. Nothing was added to the water, yet it became denser. The change in temperature was the reason.

The salt content of sea water is measured with an instrument called a *hydrometer*, which is a sealed glass tube weighted at the bottom and with a scale of calibration at the thin upper end (Figure 36). An accurate hydrometer is one that has been *standardized*—tested against a sample of sea water of known salt content and a temperature of 59 F (15 C), which is the standardization temperature chosen by oceanographers. Always buy hydrometers that have been standardized to NBS (National Bureau of Standards) standards; otherwise your measured values may not match the ones shown in Table 10.

Figure 36   *Hydrometer showing the meniscus.*

HOW TO USE A HYDROMETER

1. Turn off the air to the aquarium and wait until the surface of the water is calm.
2. Carefully lower the hydrometer into the aquarium The saltier the water the higher it will rise, much as a swimmer floats easier in salt water than in fresh.
3. When the hydrometer stops bobbing, take a reading at the *meniscus*, as shown in Figure 36. A reading taken from anywhere else on the instrument will be incorrect.
4. Don't forget to turn the air back on.

Specific gravity values at constant salinity and varying temperatures are given in Table 10. These are corrected values based on a standard temperature of 59 F (15 C). Proper use of the table assumes a salinity of 34‰ and that an accurate thermometer will be used, preferably calibrated in degrees centigrade.

Table 10   Specific Gravity Values of Sea Water at Various Temperatures and a Salinity of 34 ppt

Temperature, F	Temperature, C	Specific Gravity
86	30	1.021
84	29	1.021
82	28	1.022
81	27	1.022
79	26	1.022
77	25	1.023
75	24	1.023
73	23	1.023
72	22	1.023
70	21	1.024
68	20	1.024
66	19	1.024
64	18	1.025
63	17	1.025
61	16	1.025
59	15	1.025
57	14	1.025
55	13	1.026
54	12	1.026
52	11	1.026
50	10	1.026
48	9	1.026
46	8	1.027
45	7	1.027
43	6	1.027
41	5	1.027
39	4	1.027
37	3	1.027
36	2	1.027
34	1	1.027

HOW TO USE TABLE 10

1. Take the temperature of the water.
2. Take a hydrometer reading.
3. Compare the measured value against the value given in the table at the same temperature.
4. The difference in the two readings (measured versus corrected) is how much your specific gravity needs to be corrected.

EXAMPLE.   Water temperature = 70 F (21 C).
Hydrometer reading = 1.023.
The corrected value given in the table at 70 F (21 C) is 1.024, indicating that the water in the aquarium is too dilute, although still within acceptable limits (this reading is off by only −0.001).

Suppose your specific gravity value is higher than it should be for the temperature of the water. The water, in other words, is too salty. Carefully add some *aged tap water* (water that has been held for three days without animals and aerated to expel the chlorine), which should be the same temperature as the sea water in the aquarium. After adding a little, let the aquarium mix completely. A half hour or so later take another reading with the hydrometer and add more water as necessary.

If the reading is low, it means that the water is too dilute. Should you add more salt? This seems logical at first, but stop and think. How would you add such small amounts? Don't forget that you would have to add *all* the salts individually, each in its proper ratio to the others, Since this is impossible, the only way is to remove some of the fresh water instead. This is done by leaving the tank uncovered for a couple of days. Check the salt content daily, and when enough water has evaporated to bring the level back to normal, put the cover back on.

Chapter Six

Maintenance

6.1 THE MEANING OF "CLEAN"

It is impossible to remove all the dirt from an aquarium by conventional methods, and there is no reason to do so even if you could. "Tearing down" a tank used to be an accepted procedure before aquarists learned about biological filtration. The fishes would be removed and placed in another container. Next the old water would be thrown away, the gravel taken out and boiled, and the inside of the tank scrubbed thoroughly with table salt or baking soda. When everything was spotless the fishes would be returned, along with new water.

Everything about such a procedure is extremely detrimental. Moving the animals causes unnecessary stress. Washing and boiling the gravel either scours beneficial bacteria from the grain surfaces or kills them directly. So does scrubbing out the inside of the tank. When the aquarium is put back together, the biological filter must go through the conditioning period all over again before finally coming into equilibrium. To clean, as used here, means to remove excess surface detritus and algae; it does not mean to sterilize, because sterile conditions would be undesirable except under the special conditions described in Chapter 10, Section 8.

6.2 DETRITUS

The loose brown dirt lying on the gravel is not animal excretia. It is a complex substance formed by bacterial action on the organic molecules in the water.

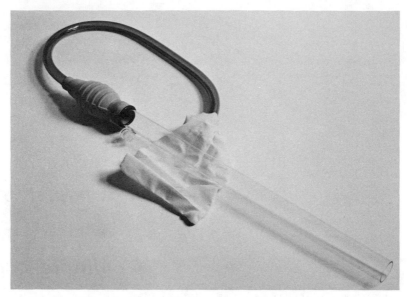

Figure 37   A vacuum tube for removing loose detritus from the surface of the filter bed.

The name for it is *detritus*. Although no evidence exists that detritus is harmful, it is unsightly and should be removed. The easiest way is to siphon it out during a partial water change or pick it up with a vacuum tube (Figure 37). Vacuum tubes are sold at most aquarium supply stores. Use separate cleaning utensils for each aquarium or soak them for a day in fresh water before reusing them.

6.3   ALGAE

Algae is not harmful to animals. In fact, many fishes and invertebrates eat it and it serves as an excellent supplement to their diet.

Algae can be removed from the glass with a sponge on a stick (Figure 38). Algae on the tank decorations and gravel should be left alone unless it becomes excessive, in which case take the decorations out and scrub them with a stiff-bristle brush and tap water. Then shake them dry and put them back. Gravel can be gently stirred to loosen surface algae. The material can then be removed with a fine-mesh net, siphon, or vacuum tube.

6.4   PARTIAL WATER CHANGES

About 10% of the aquarium water should be changed every two weeks; if this is inconvenient, a monthly 25% change will do just as well. The replacement water must be the same temperature and have the same specific gravity.

Figure 38   Sponge on a stick for cleaning aquarium glass. Each tank should have its own cleaning utensils to help prevent transfer of infectious diseases.

A partial change accomplishes three things. First, it lowers the nitrate level which in crowded aquariums sometimes exceeds the recommended ceiling of 20 ppm. When 10% of the water is discarded, so is some of the nitrate in solution.

Second, a partial water change replenishes depleted trace elements. Some trace elements are deposited with the detritus on the gravel. This means that they are no longer chemically available to the animals. Other elements are constantly being taken from solution and bound up in the tissues of growing animals.

Third, a partial change is a convenient means of removing accumulated detritus and algae. A length of air-line tubing makes a good siphon and the detritus, along with the right amount of old water, can be siphoned into a bucket or pan on the floor.

6.5   THE OUTSIDE FILTER

The outside filter needs cleaning every two weeks. A partial change of activated carbon is especially important.

HOW TO CLEAN AN OUTSIDE FILTER

1. Shut off the air to the filter unit.
2. Remove the filter fiber and wash it out under the tap. The material can be reused unless it is very dirty.
3. After rinsing the filter fiber several times, squeeze it dry.
4. Take out half the activated carbon and replace it with new material. Using all new activated carbon "shocks" the animals by taking out too much organic material at once.
5. Mix the new carbon with the old that remains in the filter. Next time use the same procedure and again replace only half the material.
6. Put back the filter fiber and spread it evenly over the activated carbon.
7. Start up the filter unit.

The Animals

Chapter Seven

≋≋≋≋≋≋≋

Which Animals

7.1 WHY CERTAIN ONES?

Typically, marine aquarists get hooked by the coral-reef fishes, and understandably so. Here are the sea's inhabitants at their peak of beauty and diversity. Nowhere in the animal kingdom—even among the birds—are there creatures to match them for sheer brilliance of color. The coral-reef fishes are the epitome of aquarium keeping, but many species, like the butterflyfishes and angelfishes, are difficult to maintain. They are definitely not recommended to any but the most experienced aquarists. One of your biggest challenges is resisting the temptation to buy the most exquisite and fragile specimens in the aquarium store. You *must* resist if you don't want to gamble away your whole investment in time and money. Nothing is more depressing than to bring home a collection of beautiful animals only to have them die within a week. The chances of this happening can be minimized simply by choosing from the groups I have listed in this chapter. These selections are based on two criteria: availability to the hobbyist and general hardiness. Within them there is enough diversity and color to satisfy anyone. Compatibility among the different groups of fishes is summarized in Table 11.

7.2 CNIDERIA

The Cnideria, previously termed Coelenterata, constitute the most primitive animals with definite tissues. There are two basic body forms: the free-swimming medusa and the sedentary polyp. Corals and sea anemones are of

71

Table 11   General Guide to Species Compatibility

Fishes	Compatible with	Incompatible with
Blennies	Blennies Damsels Filefishes Gobies Tangs Wrasses Invertebrates	Groupers Triggerfishes
Damsels	Blennies Damsels Filefishes Gobies Tangs Wrasses Invertebrates	Some damsels Groupers Triggerfishes
Filefishes	Blennies Damsels Filefishes Gobies Groupers Tangs Wrasses Most invertebrates	Triggerfishes Crustaceans
Gobies	Blennies Damsels Filefishes Gobies Tangs Wrasses Invertebrates	Groupers Triggerfishes

the latter type, which consists of a tubular body attached to a substrate, closed at one end and with tentacles surrounding the mouth. Medusae have umbrella-shaped bodies, a marginal ring of tentacles, and a centrally located mouth on the under surface.

Anemones are among the most attractive and hardy of marine aquarium animals (Plate 1). They can creep about slowly on their *basal discs* (attachment organs). If irritated or left out of the water for a time, the tentacles turn inward and the body contracts. Food is paralyzed by *nematocysts*, or minute stinging capsules located in the tentacles, and is then carried to the mouth. Digestion takes place in the digestive cavity and the undigested portions are passed back out through the mouth. Cilia on the body surfaces

Table 11   Continued

Fishes	Compatible with	Incompatible with
Groupers	Filefishes	Blennies
	Groupers	Damsels
	Tangs	Gobies
	Triggerfishes	Some groupers
	Large invertebrates	Small crustaceans
Tangs	Blennies	None
	Damsels	
	Filefishes	
	Gobies	
	Groupers	
	Tangs	
	Triggerfishes	
	Wrasses	
	Invertebrates	
Triggerfishes	Groupers	Blennies
	Tangs	Damsels
	Wrasses	Filefishes
	Most Invertebrates	Gobies
		Triggerfishes
		Crustaceans
Wrasses	Blennies	Groupers
	Damsels	
	Filefishes	
	Gobies	
	Tangs	
	Triggerfishes	
	Wrasses	
	Invertebrates	

beat constantly to keep off food particles and debris.

Despite their primitive anatomy and similarity in body plan, anemones show a remarkable variation in form. Recently fed anemones sometimes close completely while digesting food. At other times they may bend downward, stretch upward, or lie on their sides after becoming detached from the substrate. Some of these positions and body forms are illustrated in Figure 39.

The diet of most captive anemones should consist of pieces of cut fish or shrimp. Usually four feedings a week are sufficient, but if the animals appear to be shrinking they should be fed more often. With good care anemones live a long time. There are reports of some captive specimens surviving for more than 60 years.

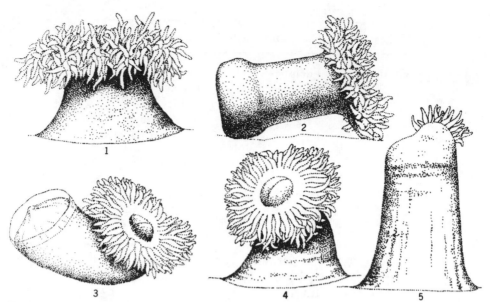

Figure 39   Stomphia, *a tropical anemone, demonstrates a complex array of behaviors:* (*1*) *normal posture;* (*2*) *resting after swimming;* (*3*) *swimming;* (*4*) *bending;* (*5*) *extending after contracting.*

7.3   CRUSTACEANS

The crustaceans are among the most abundant creatures in the sea. They belong to the phylum Arthropoda (meaning "joint-footed") and are characterized by an organic exoskeleton composed of *chiton*. This affords them a high degree of protection from predators but encases them in more or less inflexible suits of armor. Before growth can occur a crustacean must *molt*, or shed its exoskeleton. Most species have four to seven molts before attaining adulthood. Just before molting a soft new exoskeleton grows underneath the old one, loosening it and causing it to split. The animal slowly emerges from its old exoskeleton, then swallows water to expand. During this time a crustacean is vulnerable to predators, so it usually retires to a secluded spot and waits for its shell to harden.

The most commonly kept aquarium crustaceans belong to the enormous group known as the *decapods*, of which there are about 8500 species. As the name suggests, decapods are 10-legged creatures. Included among them are the crabs, shrimps, and lobsters. The latter two belong to the "long-tailed decapods;" the true crabs are lumped together as "short-tailed decapods." In general crabs make poor additions to a community aquarium. Many have cantankerous dispositions and a disconcerting habit of eating the other animals.

SHRIMPS

There are many colorful and interesting shrimps that can easily be kept in captivity. Perhaps the most conspicuous and readily available is the banded coral shrimp (Plate 2). Banded coral shrimps are nocturnal creatures that emerge from their hiding places at nightfall. A section of Caribbean reef empty of these animals during the day may teem with them at night.

Banded coral shrimps are highly territorial and are often found in pairs. If two unpaired shrimps are put together, one frequently kills the other. Be sure you have a genuine pair before putting two of them in the same aquarium tank.

LOBSTERS

Unlike their crusty northern relative the American lobster, the tropical spiny lobsters and locust lobsters are personable beasts, and small specimens make interesting additions to the aquarium. Locust lobsters are particularly mild-mannered and seldom cause the problems often experienced with other captive crustaceans (Plate 3).

Both types are scavengers that feed on animal and plant material. Sponges, mollusks, and nearly all other invertebrates except anemones, sea urchins, and sea stars (previously termed starfishes) are unsafe in their presence. Spiny lobsters (Figure 40) are equipped with powerful jaws. On Florida reefs queen conchs are sometimes found with the lips of their shells eaten away. This is the work of spiny lobsters that nibble steadily at the shell until the soft parts of the mollusk are exposed. In a 200-gal exhibit I once maintained the resident spiny lobsters constantly chewed up the larger chunks of coral gravel to get at the algae growing in the deeper crevices. Within a few months the gravel had all been turned to fine sand.

Lobsters can become cannibalistic if underfed. When one member of

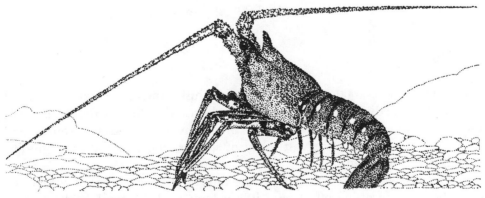

Figure 40   Spiny lobster.

the group molts, it may be eaten by the others before its new exoskeleton can harden. Lobsters about to molt should be moved to different quarters until their new shells have hardened completely. A lobster demonstrates characteristic behavior just before molting. It scratches its body constantly with its walking legs and frequently lies flat on the bottom of the aquarium with all its legs extended outward.

HERMIT CRABS

Hermit crabs are among the most interesting of all aquarium animals (Plate 4). Unlike most crabs, which are satisfied to rely on their exoskeletons for protection, hermit crabs take up residence in abandoned snail shells. Over thousands of years hermit crabs have evolved mostly "right-handed" abdomens; that is, their hindquarters curve to the right to match the right-handed whorls of most snail shells.

Despite being burdened with heavy shells, hermit crabs get around quite well. Occasionally one is found wearing a particularly thick shell, in which case movement is made only with the greatest difficulty.

As a hermit crab grows, it must move into successively larger shells. A hermit crab's posterior parts are softer than the rest of its body, so that it is vulnerable to attack from predators when completely exposed. Before moving into a new home the crab first reaches inside with one of its claws to be sure that any previous tenant has gone; then it lines up the new shell beside the old one. As quickly as possible the crab leaves the old shell and backs into the new one. Then it bobs the shell several times over its back to get the feel of it, much like a man trying on a new topcoat. If the fit is right, the animal then goes on about its business. Sometimes a different shell merely looks like a greener pasture but in truth isn't so comfortable as the original. After a few steps the crab returns and takes up residence in its old shell.

No self-respecting hermit crab can pass by an empty shell. If several empty shells are put into a tank with a hermit crab, the animal usually tries them all before reluctantly choosing one and keeping it.

7.4 MOLLUSKS

There are some 80,000 species of living mollusks and nearly as many fossil forms. They are divided into five principal classes: the chitons, the tooth shells, the snails and slugs, the clams and other bivalves, and the squids and octopuses. Considering the vast array of species, there are surprisingly few suited to the aquarium.

Chitons, which are creatures of the intertidal zone, creep monotonously over the rocks scraping off algae. Little is known about tooth shells in captivity. Clams and oysters and their kin, except for certain of the scallops

(Plate 5), make dull aquarium pets. They are difficult to feed, being filter feeders, and equally hard to spot if they die. A dead clam may, as a result, pollute an entire aquarium before it is noticed. The snails are also quick and deadly polluters if they die unnoticed. Snails make somewhat more interesting additions to the aquarium fauna, although many species have highly specialized feeding habits. For this reason it is best to read up on specific snails before buying them.

This brings us to the *cephalopods* (meaning "head-foot"). It would be difficult to find a more fascinating creature anywhere than the octopus (Figure 41). It has eight arms attached to its head, can stage escapes from sealed containers that would shame Houdini, blushes on only half its body at a time, and when cooked tastes like lobster.

The water-quality requirements of octopuses (not "octopi") are more stringent than those of many other marine animals. This makes them difficult to keep and does not recommend them to the beginning aquarist. If the water turns the least bit foul, an octopus will leave its tank and walk away, not revealing its final resting place until some hot sultry afternoon several days later. One important aspect of octopus keeping is always to have a tight-fitting lid over the aquarium. It helps if the lid is also weighted. Octopuses are unbelievably strong, so don't feel silly about putting on a few extra bricks.

Since they have no bones, octopuses can squeeze through seemingly impossible openings. In his book, *Kingdom of the Octopus*, Frank W. Lane quotes a vivid passage from the writings of N. J. Berrill, a noted authority on cephalopods:

> I once knew a naturalist who caught a fair-sized octopus, a foot or so long, and took it into a street-car, safely confined within a wicker basket. Ten minutes later came a scream from the other end of the car, and sure enough the creature had squeezed through a half-inch crack and was sitting on the lap of an hysterical passenger.

Figure 41   Octopus attacking an American lobster.

Octopuses prefer to be kept alone. If two are put into the same aquarium, one generally kills and eats the other. An octopus tank should be kept darkened at all times. Octopuses are nocturnal creatures and shun bright light. Skilled aquarists respect this and use only indirect lighting. Ample hiding places should be provided, preferably of the sort in which the animal can conceal most of its body. Clay flowerpots are excellent. Octopuses seem to prefer them to caves made of real coral.

One of the great aquarium mysteries of all time involved an octopus. (Again, Mr. Lane's book is the source.) In May 1873 the staff at the Brighton Aquarium, on the south coast of England, set up an exhibit of young lumpfish. All went well for awhile until one of the aquarists noticed that each day there was one less lumpfish. The mystery was finally solved one morning when a small but obviously well-fed octopus was found in the lumpfish tank. Somehow it had learned that the lumpfish were next door and at night would leave its own tank, crawl across the barrier separating the two exhibits, and dine on a lumpfish, always returning to its own tank before daybreak.

But the story continues. Instead of putting a lid on the tank the Brighton Aquarium staff set up nightly watches. All was quiet until suddenly one night two octopuses climbed out of the tank and moved off in different directions. This time neither went for the lumpfish exhibit. The first octopus climbed into a tank of crabs too large to be eaten and the second had to be rescued from a giant lobster.

7.5   ECHINODERMS

The echinoderms, or "spiny-skinned" animals, include the sea stars, sea urchins, sand dollars, sea cucumbers, and their relatives (Plates 6 and 7). The sea stars and sea urchins rank with the better aquarium animals, sea stars being particularly durable creatures that survive except under the worst conditions. The brittle stars, serpent stars, and basket stars are notable exceptions to the general hardiness of the echinoderms. They are delicate and are not recommended.

One might well ask how the sea stars can exist at all. They have no excretory system, no circulatory system, and a respiratory system that appears barely adequate. Yet the sea star's nervous system is among the most complex in the world of spineless animals. Its mode of locomotion is unique; it can digest its food externally by everting its stomach and releasing powerful enzymes, and it possesses uncanny powers of regeneration. Above all it is a fierce predator of the ocean floor.

Perhaps one of the most intriguing problems plaguing early marine biologists was how a sluggish creature like the sea star could open a clam. The average clam can hold its shells, or valves, shut to all but its strongest enemies. Unfortunately for the clam, few small predators are more powerful

Plate 1   Condylactis anemones (*Condylactis sp.*). Tropical Atlantic and Caribbean. (Stephen Spotte photo.)

Plate 2   Banded coral shrimp (*Stenopus hispidus*). Tropical Atlantic and Caribbean. (Photo by Carl Gage, Key Largo, FL 33038.)

Plate 3 Locust lobster
(*Scyllarides aequinoctialis*).
Tropical Atlantic and Caribbean.
(Stephen Spotte photo.)

Plate 4   Hermit crab (*Pagurus gilli*). Pacific Northwest. (Stephen Spotte photo.)

Plate 5   Flame scallop (*Lima sp.*). Tropical Atlantic and Caribbean. (Photo by Walter A. Lerchenfeld, Osborn Laboratories of Marine Science.)

Plate 6   Sea star (*Oreaster nodosus*). Red Sea. (Stephen Spotte photo.)

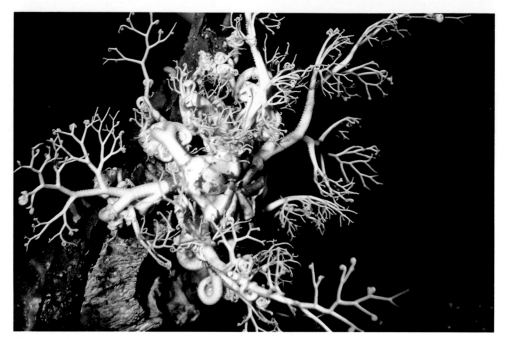

Plate 7   Basket star (*Gorgonocephalus caryi*). Pacific Northwest. (Stephen Spotte photo.)

Plate 8   Penpoint gunnel (*Apodichthys flavidus*). Pacific Northwest. (Stephen Spotte photo.)

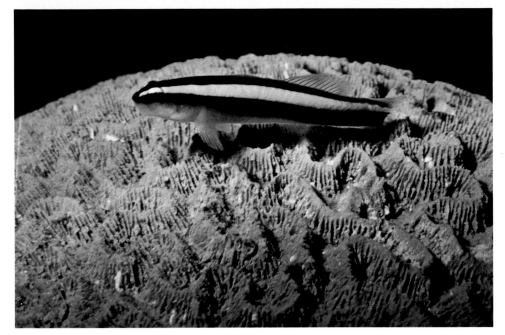

Plate 9   Neon goby (*Gobiosoma oceanops*). Tropical Atlantic and Caribbean.
(Stephen Spotte photo.)

Plate 10   Anemonefish (*Amphiprion frenatus*). Indo-Pacific. (Stephen Spotte photo.)

Plate 11 Fiji devil (*Abudefduf hemicyaneus*). Indo-Pacific. (Stephen Spotte photo.)

Plate 12   Leaf-lipped grouper (*Pogonoperca punctata*). Indo-Pacific.
(H. Douglas Kemper Jr. photo.)

Plate 13   Sailfin tang (*Zebrasoma veliferum*). Indo-Pacific.
(Stephen Spotte photo.)

Plate 14 Prickly leatherjacket (*Chaetoderma pencilligera*). Indo-Pacific. (Stephen Spotte photo.)

Plate 15 Clown wrasse (*Coris angulata*). Indo-Pacific. (Stephen Spotte photo.)

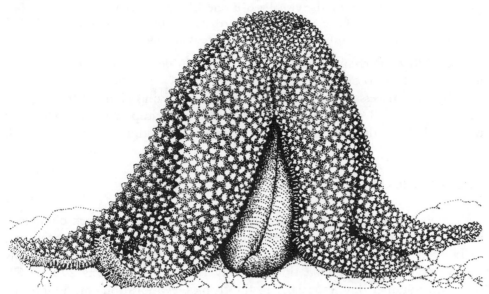

Figure 42   Sea star opening a clam.

than a sea star. It takes about 10 lb of steadily applied pressure to force open a clam. When a sea star finds a clam, it crawls over it, assumes a humped position (Figure 42), and starts to apply a strong pull on each valve. As soon as the valves open a crack, the sea star slips its stomach inside and digests the hapless clam in its own shell.

Many animals are able to shed appendages when an unpleasant stimulus is applied. This ability is called *autotomy* and is a common protective device among lower animals. If a predator grabs an arm, for instance, the arm is dropped and the animal escapes and eventually regenerates a new one. When an electric shock is applied to certain sea stars, all five arms leave the body (central disc) and walk away. In time the central disc regenerates five new arms. In some species each wandering arm, in turn, regenerates four new arms and a central disc. Years ago oyster fishermen, enraged at the damage caused by sea stars, would tear them in half and throw them back into the sea. It was later proved that each piece subsequently regenerated into a whole animal, resulting in an increase in the sea star population instead of a decline.

The sea star moves along by means of a hydraulic system. At the base of each walking structure is a tiny water sac, which leads into a stalk that terminates in a suction cup. The three structures together make up the tube foot. When the sac contracts, water is forced through the stalk, causing it to straighten. When the suction cup portion touches a surface, it becomes momentarily attached. Now the muscles in the stalk contract, forcing the water back into the sac. This combined activity pulls the animal forward. A. L. Burnett, an authority on echinoderms, described it like this:

The process can easily be visualized if one imagines throwing an anchor line from a boat to shore. If the anchor line contracts, the boat moves shoreward. The sea star moves by constantly throwing out hundreds of these anchors.

Primitive? Perhaps, but efficient enough to get the sea star to a clam and, once there, to open it.

It is not necessary to provide sea stars with living clams. Most captive specimens do well on diets of chopped fish and shrimp. Urchins, generally more catholic in their tastes, require an occasional feeding of plant material.

7.6   BLENNIES AND GOBIES

Tidepools are those shallow depressions above the low tide mark often seen along rocky coastlines. High tides inundate them, but they remain standing as isolated pockets when the tide goes out. At midday when the tide is low the water temperature in a tidepool may rise by as much as 20 F (7 C). On a hot summer day, especially in the tropics, evaporation can double the salt content.

Tidepool animals must be unusually hardy to survive in such an environment. For this reason two groups of fishes—the tidepool blennies and gobies—are ideal for the aquarium. Besides tolerating the adverse conditions just described, some can even stay out of water for hours at a time. In the tropics there are tidepool blennies and gobies that seem to be evolving into terrestrial animals. At low tide they leap from rock to rock faster than a man can run. Specimens collected by ichthyologists have been found with spiders and other small land-dwelling animals in their stomachs, proof that they actively feed on land.

Nearly a hundred years ago a marine biologist living in Topsham, England, made some of the earliest observations of the phenomenon now recognized as the biological clock. His subject was a common tidepool blenny. The fish behaved calmly enough when first placed in a bowl of sea water, but after a few hours it became restless and repeatedly tried to jump out. When a stone was placed in the bowl, the blenny climbed onto it at regular intervals. These actions corresponded exactly with local tidal rhythms. When the tide was high, the fish stayed submerged. At low tide it climbed onto its rock and stayed out of the water until the sea outside was again on the rise. The scientist kept this particular blenny for many months. During the entire time it never again saw the ocean, yet its behavior stayed perfectly in step with tidal changes.

A gunnel, an eel-like blenny, is shown in Plate 8.

Gobies range in size from less than an inch to about two feet. The shortest living vertebrate is a freshwater goby from the Philippines, first described in 1927. This tiny fish reaches a maximum length of $\frac{7}{16}$ in. (11 mm), or about the same size as a healthy mosquito larva.

Figure 43   Hairy blenny.

For droll looks and bizarre behavior no group of fishes can top the gobies. Nearly everything they do is unfishlike. They roll their eyes, turn their heads from side to side, and usually hop wherever they want to go instead of swimming. When a goby is offered a live worm, it dashes from its hiding place, seizes the victim, and shakes it vigorously like a terrier shaking a rat.

Certain gobies in the tropical Pacific live in burrows in association with snapping shrimps. The shrimps toil around the clock excavating sand and debris to keep the burrow from collapsing while the gobies do nothing but eat and loaf about the entrance.

It is sometimes difficult to tell the blennies and the gobies apart. Blennies have a long dorsal fin extending from just behind the head all the way to the tail (Figure 43). Gobies have two dorsal fins and often a tiny suction cup underneath, formed by the edges of the pelvic fins. The cup is used to cling to rocks and other stationary objects.

Gobies form the largest family of marine fishes. Often differences among species are slight and it takes an experienced ichthyologist to identify them. The neon goby (Plate 9) is especially recommended as an aquarium fish.

7.7   DAMSELFISHES

The damselfishes are almost perfect aquarium fishes. They are small, lively, colorful, and relatively inexpensive, but perhaps best of all they are hardy.

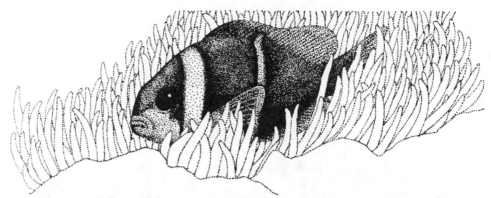

Figure 44   Anemonefish resting among the tentacles of an anemone.

The most famous of the damsels are the clownfishes, or anemonefishes, which can live with impunity among the deadly tentacles of sea anemones (Plate 10 and Figure 44).

For many years the nature of this strange relationship was a mystery. The anemonefish evidently gained sanctuary from predators, but how could it survive the anemone's sting? Was it immune? Until recently no one knew for sure just how the protective mechanism worked, but now there is proof that the anemonefish coats itself with mucus from the anemone, thereby masking its own presence.

An anemonefish must go through an "acclimation ritual" before it can live in safety with an anemone; otherwise it will be killed and eaten just like any other fish. The ritual goes something like this. The fish cautiously approaches the anemone. It may nibble at the end of a tentacle or brush lightly against an outer tentacle. The anemone stings the fish, but because only the tip of its tentacle is touched the sting is not severe. The fish gradually works its way closer, each time brushing a tentacle and receiving a mild sting, but jumping back in time to avoid fatal contact. Sometimes the anemonefish performs a little dance above its anemone. It bobs up and down, barely touching its pelvic fins to the tentacles. Gradually it works its way deeper into the anemone. By this time the anemone is stinging the fish less and less. Its behavior becomes passive and the tentacles relax. Finally the fish is able to dive at will into the center of the anemone, or burrow roughly across it without receiving any sting at all. Acclimation is now complete. It has taken about an hour.

Other members of the damselfish family are noted for their aggressiveness. The beaugregory, the dusky damsel, and the threespot damsel—all native to the Caribbean—have been known to attack human beings. If a scuba diver accidently invades the area in which a damselfish is guarding its nest, the inch-long fish instantly attacks, often grabbing a single hair on an arm or leg and tugging with the determination of a bulldog. Damselfishes from the tropical Pacific (Plate 11) behave in much the same way.

This pugnacious attitude is probably the damselfish's only drawback as an aquarium fish. With the exception of the anemonefishes, which are generally peaceful, damsels do not get along well together and care should be taken not to put too many of one species in the same tank.

7.8 SEA BASSES

The "serranids," or sea basses, are hardy and interesting aquarium fishes. Some of them live in captivity for many years and attain large size. They have two unnerving habits, however: digging up the gravel in the filter bed and eating smaller tankmates.

The most commonly kept sea basses are the groupers (Plate 12). Any aquarium containing these fishes must have clefts and other hiding places readily available to minimize digging. If not, groupers simply go about making their own facilities, often shoving all the gravel into one corner. This exposes the filter plate and interferes with normal filtration. Chunks of coral stacked one on top of another or a random scattering of clay flowerpots make good grouper houses.

If other species are kept in the same aquarium, a general rule is to be certain that they are equal in size to the largest grouper. This is the only assurance they won't get swallowed some dark night.

7.9 SURGEONFISHES

The surgeonfishes get their name from the sharp spines located on either side of the body just in front of the tail. The spines open forward. When not extended, they fold into grooves flush with the rest of the body surface.

Surgeonfishes (some members of the group are called "tangs") are probably the most herbivorous of the commonly kept aquarium fishes (Plate 13). Most can exist on a strictly vegetable diet, although it is still best to feed them mainly on animal flesh, supplemented with vegetable matter.

Socially, surgeons are peaceful and rarely cause trouble with the other inhabitants of the aquarium.

7.10 TRIGGERFISHES AND FILEFISHES

The "triggers" and "files" are strange related fishes common to all tropical seas of the world. They are slow-swimming, mostly solitary animals and entirely carnivorous, though an occasional specimen will accept vegetable matter in captivity.

The outstanding feature held in common by these two groups is the peculiar arrangement of the first two dorsal spines. The first spine is longer and can be erected. The second slides forward and locks the first into place. The smaller second spine, acting as a trigger, must then be released before the first can fold back into normal position. The spine is usually erected when the animal is disturbed.

The first dorsal spine of the filefishes (Plate 14) is normally placed forward of the eyes. In triggers it is behind the eyes. The name "filefish" has

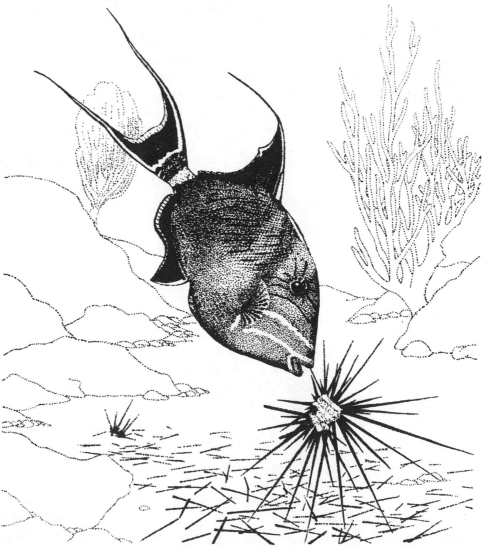

Figure 45   Queen triggerfish eating a sea urchin.

nothing to do with the trigger mechanism but refers instead to the texture of the skin and scales.

Only very small specimens of either group do well in the home aquarium. If there is too little room, they simply erect their spines and lie down on their sides, moving only at feeding time.

Triggers in particular may be highly belligerent toward one another, and two of the same species often fight. Unrelated fishes are in danger of being killed and eaten unless ample hiding places are provided. The mouths of these fishes, although small, contain strong sharp teeth capable of cracking open the spiny tests of sea urchins (Figure 45) or leisurely chopping other fishes to bits.

7.11 WRASSES

Among the most varied and colorful denizens of the coral reef are the wrasses, a large group of fishes numbering some 600 species. Often there is a startling difference between the color patterns of a juvenile and those of its parents. Early ichthyologists, in fact, classified many juveniles and adults as different species. Males and females, too, are sometimes differently colored.

Coris angulata (Plate 15) loses its juvenile spots as it matures, becoming a more solid color. In the bluehead wrasse certain males are the only ones to attain the distinctive blue head and green body. Juveniles and females stay yellow.

Wrasses swim with a characteristic dipping and gliding motion, using mainly the pectoral fins. This gives them the appearance of seagoing sparrows. At night most wrasses burrow in the gravel, and not even the keen eye of an experienced aquarist can find them without stirring up the filter bed. Some wrasses use this burrowing ability to escape from predators and can dive into the gravel and disappear in a split second.

Chapter Eight

≈≈≈≈≈≈≈≈≈≈

New Animals

8.1 BRINGING THEM HOME

The fishes and invertebrates you buy in a store have everything going against them. From their moment of capture they have been banged and battered, subjected to foul water, chilled or overheated, starved, and gawked at by human beings. The fact they are alive at all is a tribute to their endurance.

Aha! you protest. My dealer gives his animals only the best of care. Maybe. But even so, that doesn't account for capture methods used by some fish collectors or for indifferent handling by butterfingered freight agents. It has been my experience that animals finally appearing in a retailer's store are only a small percentage of the number originally taken from the sea. I would be surprised, in fact, if the survivors represent even 1%.

This tells you something: the animals you buy are in need of immediate attention. They cannot wait in a cold automobile while you stop at the supermarket. They must be brought home as quickly as possible and introduced into a stable environment. If you have resisted the temptation to buy any animals before everything at home is ready, you stand a better chance of keeping them alive.

8.2 HOW TO PICK HEALTHY ANIMALS

One secret to being a successful marine aquarist is picking healthy animals right from the start. Fishes in particular have telltale signs that indicate they aren't feeling well. You are ahead if you can spot them in the dealer's tanks and avoid buying questionable specimens.

FISHES

Color. The colors of a healthy fish are bright and clear. A fish with faded colors could be suffering from something simple, like being kept over a light-colored bottom, or from something complex, like any number of diseases. Since you can't be sure of the cause, don't buy it.

Skin Condition. The skin should be clear. Fishes are covered by mucus which acts as a first line of defense against invading disease organisms. If the mucus has been stripped away in places, as sometimes happens during handling, the fish is left vulnerable to infections. The skin should therefore be free of any blemishes. There should be no discolored or whitish patches over the body or the eyes. Such light-colored areas are indicative of disease-producing bacteria or fungi. White spots about the size of pinheads may be the encysted stages of pathogenic protozoans.

Breathing and Swimming. You don't have to be an expert to tell when a fish is breathing heavily or when its swimming is aimless and erratic. Rapid breathing can be caused by several things: insufficient oxygen, ammonia poisoning, parasites covering the gills, and so forth. When a fish has difficulty in maintaining its equilibrium, it could be the result of a sudden temperature change that has resulted in *thermal shock*. It could also be caused by disease.

General Behavior. A fish is too stereotyped a creature for its behavior to be altered drastically by captivity. Unless it is continually stressed, it will soon resume normal patterns of feeding, resting, and defending a territory. A fish that hangs about in the upper corners of the tank and has ragged fins is showing signs of not being able to hold a territory. If it is confined in the same tank too long, it will eventually be killed by its tankmates. Purchase the winner of the territorial dispute, not the loser.

Starvation. A fish can have a full belly and still be starving to death. In nature, many small fishes feed throughout the day, endlessly ingesting tiny amounts of food. If they go for more than a day or two in captivity without eating, most are doomed to eventual starvation, even if they resume feeding. These fishes can easily be spotted by examining the area of the back just above the backbone. If the flesh is compressed, as if someone had picked up the fish and pinched it between his fingers, then it is suffering from starvation and there isn't much anyone can do for it. This principle is illustrated in Figure 46.

If a fish can pass all the above criteria on the positive side, it is a good risk. If it fails even one, don't buy it, no matter how attractive it might be otherwise.

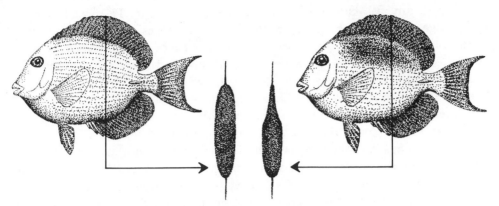

Figure 46   Well-fed versus a starved fish. The upper body of the well-fed fish (left) *is filled out, as shown in the cross section. In the starved fish* (right), *the cross section illustrates how the upper body becomes emaciated even though the fish may have a full belly.*

INVERTEBRATES

Invertebrates are more difficult to judge. Their great diversity of form has resulted in equally wider-ranging behaviors. Also, being lower on the evolutionary scale has deprived them of an extensive repertoire of behaviors—at least any that nonspecialists can recognize. This means that a healthy invertebrate often looks the same as a sick one.

Learn as much as you can about the normal behavior of the species you wish to keep. A fast-moving crab, for example, should scuttle across the tank when you touch it. An anemone should be extended unless it has recently eaten, and urchins and sea stars should be actively hunting for food.

8.3   HOW TO CAPTURE ANIMALS IN THE TANK

Now that you have selected your animals in the dealer's tank, the next step is to get them out with a net, right? Wrong. Nets probably kill more marine animals—especially fishes—than any other tool available to aquarists. Death from a net can come in many insidious ways.

First, fishes can easily see a net. In an effort to avoid capture they dash madly about the tank bumping into walls and decorations. This causes immediate damage to their body surfaces and exposes them to later infections.

Second, many rough-scaled species become entangled in the webbing. At the very least these specimens lose protective mucus; frequently they lose entire scales as well. When you attempt to untangle, say, a triggerfish that has erected its dorsal spines in the net, further damage is caused either by gripping the creature too tightly and bruising it or by directly transferring bacteria from your hands to the newly abraded areas on its skin.

Third, any fish caught in a net suffers eye damage. In most fishes the eyes bulge out, making them among the first places to become injured. Many blind aquarium fishes get that way because of nets, not as a result of some mysterious disease, as is generally thought. Imagine for a moment your own lidless eyes being scraped across the webbing of even the softest net.

The *only* correct way to catch a fish is to use a plastic bag—the same bag it will be carried home in. With a bag there is less stress during capture, since the translucent polyethylene is difficult for a fish to see and therefore avoid. No mucus is rubbed off as with a net. Scales are not lost and eyes and skin are not abraded. The animal never leaves the water. Also, a new bag is certainly more sterile than a net that has been used to catch different fishes—usually in different tanks—day after day, and there is less chance of disease transfer. Last but not least, a fish "untouched by human hands" always stands a better chance of survival.

8.4   ACCLIMATING NEW ANIMALS

The acclimation period of a new animal is a critical time. It is going from one environment to another or, if you prefer, from one set of living conditions to the next. Unless it is a tidepool species it is rarely, if ever, required to adjust to changes of such magnitude in the wild. Acclimation must be accomplished smoothly and with a minimum of stress.

LIGHTS

Lighting in the room should be dim when you unpack your new animals. The reflector over the tank and any ceiling lights should be off. Fishes sometimes go into *photo shock;* that is, the sudden flashing of a bright light on a fish already adjusted to semidarkness can fatally interrupt some of its vital physiological processes.

TEMPERATURE

Ideally, you should call your dealer the day before buying your animals and get the temperatures in his tanks; then adjust yours to match. Temperature is one of the most critical factors affecting newly acquired animals and its importance should never be overlooked.

FLOTATION

Floating the animals in the tank in their plastic bags is a procedure that has come under criticism from experienced aquarists, probably with justification. They point out that many gases can pass freely from the aquarium water through the bag and also that few people allow enough time for floating to do some good. Although the critics are right on both counts, flotation is still the best technique available for acclimating new animals to different environments.

HOW TO ACCLIMATE NEW ANIMALS

1. Open each bag after it has been put into the tank and drop an air-stone into it. The oxygen content must not be allowed to decline nor the amount of carbon dioxide to increase. Mild aeration prevents both from happening.
2. Float the bags for at least an hour. Every 15 minutes or so add a little tank water to each bag. This gradually gets the fishes used to differences in chemical content.
3. When the water temperatures in the bags and in the tank have been the same for at least 30 minutes, gently tip the bags and let the animals swim out. Do not turn the bags upside down and pour the specimens into the tank because such a technique creates needless stress.
4. Keep the lights dimmed for the rest of the day. If the animals show signs of having adjusted before the day is out, try giving them a very light feeding.

Chapter Nine

Nutrition and Feeding

9.1 MEANING OF NUTRITION

Nutrition is the benefit an animal gets from the things it eats. If nutrition is adequate, the animal may live and flourish; if not, it declines and dies.

Food is utilized by animals in three ways. First, a portion of it is burned immediately to supply energy. Second, a part may be converted to animal starch and stored in the tissues to supply energy in the future. Third, some may be used for building protoplasm—either replacing wornout cells or adding new ones. When the production of new cells exceeds weight lost through metabolic processes, the bulk of the animal increases. This is what we call *growth*.

Animals cannot grow without a source of energy. The growth of bone and muscle and skin and scales requires energy in addition to the building materials themselves. Biological energy is measured in terms of calories. When calories are chemically burned in the body, the energy that is produced is equal to the heat energy produced when they are literally burned. The definition of a *calorie* is the amount of heat necessary to raise the temperature of one gram of water one degree centigrade. If we compare a living organism to a gasoline engine, food would be analogous to gasoline and calories to octane. Some foods, like some fuels, give higher "performance" than others. In other words, their energy potential is greater.

Animals, like engines, have different energy requirements. A high-octane fuel is wasted on a small, low-rpm engine. In like manner, high-calorie foods are of less value to a sedentary flounder than to a fast-swimming damselfish. Young fishes invariably need more calories per body weight in a given period of time than older fishes of the same species. Young fishes are adding new tissue rapidly and must be fed several times daily to receive their caloric requirements.

All animals are classed as *carnivorous, herbivorous,* or *omnivorous,* depending on whether their diets consist of animal material, plant material, or both.

In fishes the length of the intestine is closely related to diet. Carnivores have short, straight intestines. Herbivores have extremely long intestines. The intestines of omnivores are generally intermediate in length. Herbivores have evolved longer intestines because the digestion of plant material takes longer. Also, the conversion factor when plant material is used as food is always lower. In other words, more of it must be eaten to produce growth. This makes animal flesh more efficient as a food source.

9.2 BASIC DIETARY CONSTITUENTS

Animals require five basic constituents in their diets: proteins, carbohydrates, fats, vitamins, and minerals.

PROTEINS

Proteins are typically the most limiting of all the dietary constituents. The others permit a certain margin of error, but when protein intake declines below minimum requirements growth and tissue replacement stop.

Protein requirements vary according to species. As we have just seen, animals consume animal and plant material in different amounts. Carnivores need a greater percentage of protein than herbivores. Insofar as fishes are concerned, none can tolerate a diet in which the protein level falls below 6%.

There are two types of protein and enormous possible numbers of each type, depending on how the molecules are arranged. Each species of animal, in fact, is composed of its own characteristic proteins. Basically, there are the *simple proteins,* which give only amino acids when broken down, and the *conjugated proteins,* which break down into amino acids, plus other substances.

Amino acids are the basic components of protein. Many of them can be synthesized by animals, but a few are either utilized more rapidly than they can be produced or they cannot be synthesized at all. These are called the *essential amino acids,* since they are essential to the animal's health and must be supplied in its food.

Proteins, as such, cannot be utilized directly; they must first be broken down into their component amino acids by the process of *hydrolysis,* which refers to chemical decomposition as the result of reacting with water. Both simple and conjugated proteins are "hydrolyzed," then selectively reassembled in different combinations to form the proteins peculiar to the species of animal that is using them.

Ideally, any artificial diet for fishes should contain the essential amino acids in their proper quantities. Unfortunately, these quantities have been determined for only a few commercially important freshwater species, notably the salmonids, carp, and channel catfish. The correct amino acids must therefore be delivered in their nonhydrolyzed "crude" forms, which are commonly shrimp and fish meal, fish flesh, liver, beef heart and muscle, and so forth.

CARBOHYDRATES

Carbohydrates are substances composed of carbon, hydrogen, and oxygen, usually with the hydrogen and oxygen in a 2 to 1 ratio.

Carbohydrates have their origin in the plant kingdom. Among animals only a few protozoa can synthesize carbohydrates; the rest must obtain them with their food.

Plants commonly store food as starch. When plant material is eaten by an animal, it is broken down into sugars before being assimilated. Some of it may be stored as animal starch and used as future sources of energy. Starch is probably less critical in the diet than proteins or fats, but herbivores, and to a lesser degree omnivores, may require more starch in their diets. Feeding some plant material several times a week will suffice.

FATS

The lipids, commonly called fats, are essential components in the diets of all animals. Fats are either *saturated* or *unsaturated*, the difference being in how the molecules are joined together. Fish fats are essentially unsaturated, whereas those of the higher vertebrates are saturated.

Little is known about the digestion of fats by invertebrates. In fishes the amount required varies appreciably. Carnivores appear to be less tolerant of high fat levels in the diet than herbivorous or omnivorous species. Generally fishes can more easily digest unsaturated fats. This means that the fats in beef, pork, and other meats may be incompletely digested.

VITAMINS

Vitamins, like water, minerals, and dissolved gases, are classed as nonenergy substances. They have no caloric value and therefore cannot be converted into energy. Vitamins serve as catalysts for many biochemical reactions occurring in the tissues of living animals.

The vitamin requirements of aquatic animals are poorly understood. In fact, with the exception of a few commercially important species, virtually nothing is known. In general, fishes in the wild obtain sufficient vitamins from the foods they eat, since only tiny amounts of each are necessary. In captivity artificial diets are sometimes deficient in one or more vitamins. It is thought that many diseases of captive fishes and invertebrates may be the indirect result of vitamin deficiencies. The infectious organisms that cause the diseases are actually secondary invaders, which take advantage of the already weakened condition of the animals.

The safest means of preventing vitamin deficiencies is to offer your animals a wide variety of foods. This is the "shot-gun" approach. What may be lacking in one food, in other words, is compensated for at the next feeding when you offer something different.

MINERALS

Minerals play a multitude of roles in living tissue. Many are used in the synthesis of amino acids and proteins. Calcium, magnesium, and phosphorus are vital in bone formation. Others, such as iron, copper, and cobalt, are necessary for hemoglobin production in the blood. Still others aid in maintaining cellular pH and ionic balance across cell membranes.

A mineral deficiency is an unlikely occurrence in a marine aquarium. The tissues of the animals are continuously bathed in a complex solution of minerals. Natural foods supplement the uptake of minerals from the environment.

9.3   TYPES OF FOODS

Types of food may be arbitrarily broken down into three categories: natural, prepared, and live.

NATURAL FOODS

Natural foods, as described here, refer to animal and plant tissue, either fresh or frozen. Many kinds of meat, fish, and vegetables could come under this classification, but only four are discussed.

Fish Flesh. The flesh of fishes is the most usable form of protein to feed to other fishes. Each species of animal, you will remember, is composed of its own characteristic amino acids. When an animal ingests protein, it must convert this food to amino acids before it can be assimilated. Since fishes are more closely related to one another than to chickens, cows, or pigs, it is easier for them to convert fish proteins than those in fowl, beef, or pork. Also, the saturated fats in meat are often difficult for fishes to digest. Meat should be fed sparingly or not at all.

Any species of fish can be used as food if it is not too oily. Four kinds to

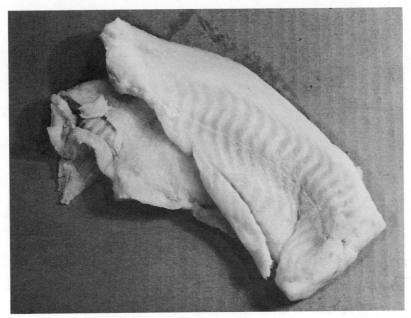

Figure 47   Frozen fish fillets sold in supermarkets are a main staple in the diets of marine aquarium animals.

avoid are herring, mackerel, menhaden, and mullet. Frozen fish fillets sold in supermarkets are perfectly suitable as long as they have not been breaded or precooked (Figure 47). Ocean perch, haddock, and halibut, for example, are all excellent. Fish flesh should be a staple in the diet of your animals.

HOW TO PREPARE FROZEN FISH

1. Keep the fish in the freezer until shortly before feeding time.
2. Cut off a chunk suitable for a single feeding and let it partially thaw at room temperature.
3. When it is fairly soft, cut it into pieces.
4. Let the pieces thaw completely before feeding them to your aquarium animals.

Shrimp. Shrimp is another staple. The shrimp to use is the one commonly sold for human consumption. It is sometimes called "green shrimp." Be sure it is raw, as shown in Figure 48. Cooking often reduces the nutritional value of foods.

Figure 48   Raw shrimp is another excellent food.

HOW TO PREPARE FROZEN SHRIMP

1. Keep the shrimp frozen until shortly before feeding.
2. Take out the amount you can use at one feeding and let it thaw partially at room temperature.
3. When it is fairly soft, remove the heads, legs, and shells and cut the flesh into pieces.
4. Let the pieces thaw completely before feeding them to your aquarium animals.

Frozen Brine Shrimp. Frozen brine shrimp make a good supplementary food but should not be used as a major constituent in the diet. Always buy the frozen *adult* brine shrimp (Figure 49); newly hatched shrimp are too small for many aquarium animals. Frozen brine shrimp can be purchased at most shops that sell aquarium supplies.

Figure 49   Frozen brine shrimp.

HOW TO PREPARE FROZEN BRINE SHRIMP

1. Just before feeding time take the frozen block of shrimp out of the freezer and chop off a small piece.
2. Drop it into a glass partly filled with lukewarm tap water, as shown in Figure 50.
3. After the piece has thawed completely and the shrimp have separated, drain off the water.
4. Wash the shrimp with another change of tap water.
5. Drain and feed. Sometimes it is easier to scoop up a little of the tank water in the glass and then pour the shrimp gently into the tank.

Figure 50   Thaw frozen brine shrimp by dropping a chunk into a glass partly filled with lukewarm tap water.

Figure 51   Frozen whole-leaf spinach provides the vegetable matter required by many omnivores and herbivores.

Figure 52   Closeup view of a dried flake food.

Spinach. Frozen leaf spinach is the fourth staple in the diet. It is an excellent source of plant material for herbivores and omnivores. It, too, can be bought at the supermarket (Figure 51). Prepare it in the same manner as frozen brine shrimp.

PREPARED FOODS

As used here, the term "prepared foods" refers to packaged dry foods. It is extremely doubtful whether any of them constitutes a complete diet. Dry foods should therefore be used only to supplement the main diet of fish, shrimp, and spinach.

There are many types of dry food on the market. The one shown in Figure 52 is typical. Some come as flakes, others as powders, and still others as tiny pellets. Flake foods may be the most convenient because the uneaten portion can be easily removed with a net. Avoid those brands that are composed largely of insect parts and other materials of doubtful food value.

LIVE FOODS

It is a good idea always to have a supply of live food on hand. As we saw in Chapter 5, the first few days after a new animal has been introduced into the aquarium are critical. If the animal has been underfed, it is important to start it feeding as quickly as possible. Many newly captured animals and animals that have been starved will accept only live food at first. There is little advantage in starving them further in hopes of teaching them to take natural or prepared foods.

Smaller live foods, such as newly hatched brine shrimp, are ideal for feeding to certain invertebrates and small fishes. The *filter feeders* (e.g., barnacles, feather-duster worms, and live corals) actually feed by filtering particles of food from the water. This makes it difficult to offer them the same variety of foods that may be fed to the other animals, and therefore it is imperative that they be given the most nutritious substances available.

Live-food organisms serve as living capsules of nutrition. They are composed of proteins, carbohydrates, and fats, but perhaps more important they often contain a concentration of vitamins. Moreover, the vitamins in the tissues of living organisms cannot dissipate into the water, as sometimes happens with natural and prepared foods.

MAKING YOUR OWN FISH FOOD

Aquarists with a culinary flair may enjoy making their own fish food. Animal gelatin is used as a binding agent to hold together the various ingredients and keep them from dissipating in the water (Figure 53). The formula is highly versatile and aquarists can alter the components with little difficulty. Trout meal can be obtained from animal feed wholesale or retail outlets. Dried flake food can be substituted, although trout meal is probably superior in nutritional value. You can buy animal gelatin at the supermarket.

Assemble the ingredients listed in Table 12; then follow the steps below. The finished cost of the artificial food is about 15 cents per pound.

Table 12   Ingredients for Homemade Fish Food[a]

	%	Quantity
Water	53	8¾ cups (1590 ml)
Trout diet in meal form	25	5 oz (750 g)
Fish or shrimp	12	12 oz (360 g)
Animal gelatin	10	10 oz (300 g)

[a] Makes about 6¼ lb (3000 g)

Figure 53   The ingredients needed to make your own fish food: raw shrimp or fish, animal gelatin, a thermometer, a measuring cup, and trout meal. Not shown are the blender, mixer, and cooling tray.

HOW TO MAKE FISH FOOD

1. Drain the flavoring ingredients (fish or shrimp) and blend them in an electric blender. Add a half cup of water.
2. Dissolve the animal gelatin in $8\frac{1}{4}$ cups of hot water at 200 F (93 C). Blend the solution with an electric mixer until it becomes smooth and free of lumps.
3. Cool to 150 F (66 C).
4. Add the flavoring ingredients and the meal to the dissolved gelatin. Mix at low speed.
5. Pour into shallow trays and cool. Store the mix in the refrigerator until needed. The final product is rubbery and can be shredded or chopped into appropriate sizes before feeding.

9.4 RAISING LIVE FOOD

BRINE SHRIMP

HOW TO HATCH BRINE SHRIMP

1. Fill a clean 1-gal jug three-fourths full with aged tap water, 70 to 80 F (21–27 C).
2. Add six level tablespoons of table salt (NaCl) through a funnel.
3. Add one level teaspoon of brine shrimp eggs through the funnel. (The eggs can be purchased at aquarium supply stores.)
4. Drop in an airstone and aerate the water vigorously until the eggs hatch (one or two days), as shown in Figure 54. Larval brine shrimp, greatly magnified, are shown in Figure 55.
5. After hatching, remove the airstone and let the empty eggshells settle to the bottom of the jug.
6. Brine shrimp are strongly attracted to light, so it is easy to concentrate them in one area before trying to remove them. This can be done by shining a light at one side of the jug, near the top.
7. When most of the shrimp are concentrated under the light, siphon them into another container through a length of tubing.
8. Dump out the water and eggshells, rinse out the jug under the tap, and start another culture. When two jugs are kept going, one of them can be emptied every other day, thus assuring a steady supply of shrimp.

Baby brine shrimp are too small for many animals. Larger fishes, for example, require larger forms of live food. For them adult brine shrimp are ideal, since they grow to a quarter of an inch in length. An adult brine shrimp culture is simple to maintain once it has been started. Leftover newly hatched shrimp can be added periodically. Often the adult shrimp will mate and reproduce, thereby helping to sustain the culture.

Once they become adults, brine shrimp can be kept alive much longer if they are refrigerated. Pour them into a shallow baking pan and set the pan on a shelf in the refrigerator or use the vegetable crisper as a holding tray (Figure 56). Put an airstone in the water. The source of air can be an inexpensive vibrator compressor that is also kept in the refrigerator. Run the cord from the compressor between the molding of the refrigerator door and plug it into a nearby wall outlet. Keep the temperature inside the refrigerator about 50 F (10 C).

Figure 54   Brine shrimp eggs can be hatched in any suitable container, such as this gallon jug. Simply add the eggs to a brine solution and drop in an airstone. Hatching time is about 24 hours.

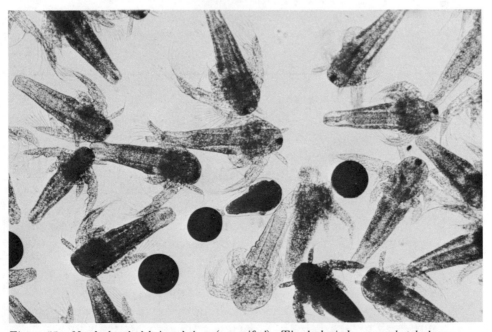

Figure 55   Newly hatched brine shrimp (magnified). The dark circles are unhatched eggs.

Figure 56   Adult brine shrimp stay alive longer if kept cool. In the arrangement shown here the shrimp are kept in the vegetable crisper of a refrigerator and aerated by a compressor on an upper shelf.

HOW TO RAISE BRINE SHRIMP

1. Hatch three flat tablespoons of brine shrimp eggs by the method just described.
2. Dissolve 20 oz (600 g) of table salt (NaCl) in about 10 gal of tap water in a plastic garbage can. When the salt has completely dissolved, adjust the specific gravity to 1.025.
3. Add 2 oz. (60 g) of epsom salt ($MgSO_4$).
4. Drop an airstone into the can and aerate the water vigorously for two days.
5. Add the larval shrimp.
6. Add two flat tablespoons (about 30 g) of a dog vitamin premix (sold by the pound at most pet stores) to the can each day.
7. The shrimp grow to adulthood in about three weeks if the temperature is 70 to 80 F (21–27 C). Remove them as needed with a net.

EARTHWORMS

Earthworms are an inexpensive and easy to raise form of live food. Earthworms can be collected from almost any patch of ground during the warmer months. The adults can be used to "seed" the worm bed and form the nucleus of a brood stock. If the worms are properly cared for and enough adults are always present, the bed will be self-sustaining. Your only job will be to feed and water them.

Earthworms burrow by pushing the soil particles outward with their front ends. Sometimes they eat their way through the soil, so it is always a good idea to "strip" a worm before washing it, chopping it up, and feeding it to your aquarium animals. A worm is stripped by holding it firmly at the head end and squeezing it between the fingers of your other hand along its entire length, as shown in Figure 57. Stripping forces out the ingested earth and partly digested food and helps keep the aquarium water clean.

In nature, earthworms mate through much of the year, being most active during warm, moist weather. Earthworms are *hermaphroditic;* that is, each worm contains both male and female reproductive organs and two worms

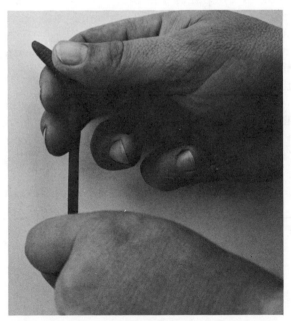

Figure 57   To "strip" an earthworm hold it between your fingers and squeeze out the partly digested earth. This prevents it from fouling the aquarium.

mate by fertilizing each other. Eggs are contained in small cocoons which are deposited in the soil. Under favorable conditions the young hatch in two to four weeks.

HOW TO RAISE EARTHWORMS

1. Select a cool, dark spot for the worm bed. A cellar or basement with a constant temperature of 60 to 70 F (15–20 C) is ideal. Most species of earthworms fare poorly at temperatures above 70 F.
2. Build a box with half- or three-quarter-inch plywood. When assembling it, screw the pieces together instead of nailing them. Almost any size will do, but a box 1 ft high $\times$ 4 ft wide $\times$ 4 ft long is convenient.
3. If you want the box to be watertight, spread a bead of silicone sealant along the edges to be joined before screwing them together. Paint the inside of the box with three coats of a good epoxy paint or polyester resin.
4. Drill a hole in the bottom near the center. This will be the emergency drain in case too much water is added by accident. The hole can be plugged from underneath with a sink or bathtub stopper.
5. Set the box on four cinder blocks, as shown in Figure 58.
6. Fill the box to a depth of 6 to 8 in. with a layer of rich loam or well decomposed mulch. Do not use sandy soil because the sand will irritate the worms' digestive tracts.
7. Add the worms and sprinkle the top of the soil with water until it is moist, *not wet*.
8. Cover the whole bed with damp burlap.
9. Feed the worms dry cornmeal. If they are fed only in one corner, they will congregate there; this makes it easier to remove them without disturbing large areas of the bed. To feed, simply lift up the burlap and sprinkle the meal on the surface of the soil (Figure 59).
10. Give the worms a little food and water two or three times a week.

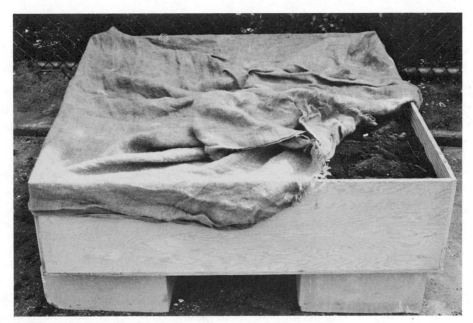

Figure 58   A worm bed set on blocks and covered with wet burlap.

Figure 59   Earthworms can be fed by sprinkling cornmeal on the surface of the bed two or three times a week.

9.5 FEEDING TECHNIQUES

HOW OFTEN TO FEED

Many animals should be fed twice daily. Small coral-reef fishes in particular do poorly if fed less often. In nature, the smaller species feed more or less constantly throughout much of the day. They dart from coral to coral, picking algae from the rocks or tiny animals trapped by the coral polyps. It is impossible, of course, to duplicate such conditions in the aquarium. Therefore, frequent feedings of small amounts of food are more beneficial than one feeding of a large amount.

Some of the invertebrates are voracious eaters. Sea urchins are noted for their appetites. Others, like anemones and sea stars, need be fed only every second or third day. The only way to be sure is to watch each animal closely until you learn its requirements.

HOW MUCH TO FEED

The old axiom used by freshwater aquarists—all the fishes will clean up in five minutes—does not often work with marine animals. In trying to find out how much this actually is, you risk polluting your aquarium by dumping in too much at once. A better way is to drop tiny amounts into the water and wait until each bit is consumed. After awhile the animals will become disinterested. You can stop at this point without having any leftover food to remove.

FEEDING

Aquarium animals must be fed with great care. Just dropping the food to them is often not good enough. In some cases one or two animals will achieve social dominance. They will harass the other creatures unmercifully and hoard most of the food at feeding time. Their tankmates will gradually starve if not attended to. A good way to circumvent this is to feed the dominant animals until they are full, then feed the others.

Different species have different feeding habits. Some food must reach the bottom for bottom-dwellers like crabs, shrimps, and blennies. Other fishes feed near the surface or in the middle of the water column. An anemone is easily fed by gently dropping a piece of fish or shrimp onto its tentacles.

Size is also important. A tiny blenny can gulp down a chunk nearly as big as its head, but a much larger tang, with its comparatively small mouth, must nibble away at a piece the same size. Other animals, notably the filter feeders, must be given their food in a special way if they are to receive enough to survive.

The aquarist, then, is faced with an interesting array of problems with respect to feeding. Feeding his animals only the most nutritious foods is not enough; he must at the same time see to it that each creature in the aquarium gets enough to eat.

FILTER FEEDERS

Filter feeders should be fed newly hatched brine shrimp. As a rule, feeding them every other day is sufficient.

The basic procedure is to remove the filter feeders from the aquarium and put them in a smaller, more confined area in which their food can be delivered to them in concentrated amounts. This gives them a chance to ingest more food and also prevents fouling the aquarium with an excess of larval brine shrimp.

HOW TO FEED FILTER FEEDERS

1. Find a container that is barely large enough to hold the filter feeders and enough sea water to cover them completely. A small aquarium tank or plastic bucket or a mixing bowl from the kitchen works well.
2. Fill the container with water from the aquarium. This is very important. Do not use new sea water or water from another aquarium. Your animals have adjusted to this particular water and changing it may cause them to stop feeding.
3. Pick up the animals and gently place them in the feeding container (Figure 60). Barnacles, feather-duster worms, and many of the smaller anemones may be attached to rocks or pieces of coral, in which case pick up the rock and all and put it in the feeding container.
4. Siphon a suitable number of newly hatched brine shrimp from the hatching jug into another container. Remove them with a fine-mesh net. Remember that the eggs were hatched in table salt and tap water—not in sea water. It could be dangerous to your animals if you dumped too much of this water into their container.
5. Place an airstone in the container and aerate the water mildly. This keeps it oxygenated and also circulates the larval shrimp.
6. Observe the filter feeders closely. At first it will be awhile before they start feeding. Handling disturbs some species. Allow them ample time to feed (about 2 hours), once they extend themselves and begin to behave normally.
7. At the end of the feeding period, take the animals out of the container and put them back into the aquarium. The amount of shrimp the animals can ingest often depends on how many are available. Ideally, put in enough to make the water in the feeding container turn cloudy with shrimp.

Figure 60   Transfer filter feeders to a container of their own water saturated with newly hatched brine shrimp. Let the animals feed for an hour or two before moving them back to the aquarium tank.

Chapter Ten

Infections and Infestations

10.1 PARASITES

By classic definition, a *parasite* is any organism that derives nutrients from the living tissues of another. This is not to be confused with predator-prey relationships in which the prey is killed and eaten. A successful parasite cannot afford such a luxury and takes only enough nourishment from its host to stay alive and reproduce. If the host dies, so does the parasite.

Coping with parasites can be one of the more discouraging aspects of aquarium keeping. Many gaps exist in our knowledge of parasitic relationships in the sea, particularly with regard to the diseases and treatment of invertebrates. Discussion in this chapter is therefore limited to parasites indigenous to fishes and then only to the most common ones.

Compounding the problem is the fact that aquarium fishes are generally more heavily parasitized than their counterparts in nature, where the vastness of the biosphere diminishes the effects of any single disease. But within the aquarium's restrictive walls there is no escape.

There are two types of infection. A *pathogenic* infection exists in a disease-producing state. In a *latent* infection the fish has more or less reached an agreement with its parasites: they still live together but the parasites are only mildly infectious. This is due to immunities built up by the fish and augmented by a healthy and stable environment. If the environment deteriorates, dissolution of the acquired immunity soon follows and the latent infection becomes pathogenic. The term "infection," incidently, is used with viruses, bacteria, protozoans, and fungi. "Infestation" refers to attacks by parasitic worms and arthropods.

The life histories of many parasites are wonderfully complex. In this respect they are among the most fascinating creatures in the animal kingdom. The animal in which a parasite takes up residence is called a *host*. The host harboring the parasite when it reaches sexual maturity is known as the *definitive* or final host. One in which the parasite lives part or all of its larval life is the *intermediate* host. A parasite can have several intermediate hosts but only one final host. It is important to note that only those parasites with direct development (i.e., those that can complete their life histories without any intermediate host) are problems in the aquarium. Others are less trouble because the odds are remote that both an intermediate and a final host could end up in the same aquarium. Subsequent discussion is thus limited to parasitic organisms that develop directly.

The outbreak of disease in the aquarium is a matter to be considered thoughtfully; aquatic animals are not amenable to treatment the way terrestrial creatures are. If we use the analogy that a fish is a solution within a solution, the disease factor suddenly becomes more complex. Is the fish to be considered alone or must we also think of the environment? If so, how much influence will the environment play on the recovery or demise of the fish?

No doubt exists about the environment's importance. This leads to the one unbendable rule for treating sick fishes: *never treat them in the aquarium.* A sick fish should be removed to another container for treatment and for one very good reason. No drug or chemotherapeutic compound is completely selective in the organisms it kills. This usually means that it destroys beneficial organisms in the filter bed along with those that are disease producing. Antibiotics are especially lethal because they are formulated specifically for use against bacteria. Nitrifiers can be completely wiped out as a result of their use. Heterotrophs, which are involved in the first stages of biological filtration, are also killed. This means that ammonia produced by the fishes cannot be converted to less toxic compounds. As it accumulates in the water, the fishes, already weakened by disease, succumb even quicker from the added stress of ammonia poisoning. You are not helping your fishes in the least by dumping such medicines into their aquarium water. Keep a small treatment tank filled with sea water for such purposes and your record of successful cures will increase markedly. You also will have a suitable environment to offer your animals after they recover, instead of one devoid of beneficial bacteria.

If you plan to treat your fishes, you should have a treatment tank in operation ahead of time, ready to go. This can be an aquarium tank of any size, provided it is equipped with clean sea water (natural or synthetic), a subgravel filter and calcareous filter gravel, and a heater and cover. Two items that you will not need are an outside filter (activated carbon adsorbs

Figure 61   A treatment tank showing the exact volume of water and the water level when the tank is full. The clay flower pots provide hiding places for sick fishes.

many forms of medication, removing them from solution) and overhead lighting.

When filling the tank, measure the exact volume of water you have added. Simply knowing that it is a "five-gallon aquarium" is not accurate enough because the gravel will displace a good part of the volume. Most formulations for treating diseases are based on the metric system, which

---

HOW TO CARE FOR SICK FISHES

1. Keep the treatment tank in semidarkness at all times.
2. Be sure that large corals or other items are placed in the treatment tank for hiding places. Clay flowerpots also make good hiding places (Figure 61).
3. Feed lightly and be sure to remove even the tiniest bits of uneaten food. Biological filtration is interrupted by many chemicals used to treat fish diseases. Some ammonia may still be produced by mineralization, however, and not be converted by nitrification. Also, some ammonia will be excreted by the fishes directly, thus adding to the general increase. Compounding this problem is the fact that diseased fishes are more susceptible to ammonia poisoning.
4. Keep the temperature constant.
5. Maintain a supply of live foods, such as adult brine shrimp.
6. Do not overcrowd.
7. Be sure each treatment tank has its own cleaning utensils so as to reduce the spread of disease.

makes it necessary to convert gallons to liters. Since there are 3.79 liters in a gallon, multiply the number of gallons by this figure. Afterward, write the volume in liters on the side of the tank with a wax pencil so you won't forget, and also draw a line at the water level (Figure 61). This allows you to compensate later for evaporation or to replace the exact volume after a water change.

10.2   VIRUSES

LYMPHOCYSTIS

Description. Perhaps the most common virus disease in fishes—both freshwater and marine—is *lymphocystis*, first detected in a European flounder in 1874. The disease is characterized by white or gray nodules that may occur on almost any part of the body. The authors of one book on fish diseases have referred to the infected area as containing ". . . . grape-like or raspberry-like growths . . . ." Such places are the skin's reaction to the invasion of the virus. Other writers described the appearance as "tapiocalike." In Europe it is sometimes called "cauliflower disease."

Pathology. The cells of the infected area become enlarged, frequently many times over (Figure 62). Generally, infection is limited to external body surfaces, as shown in Figures 63 and 64, although lesions have also been found in the gills, heart, intestine, and other organs. Lymphocystis is not fatal,

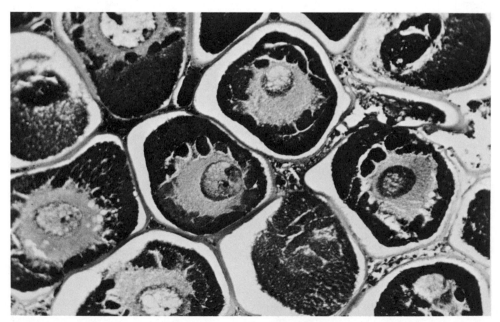

Figure 62   Cells of a marine fish infected with lymphocystis disease (magnified 231 X).

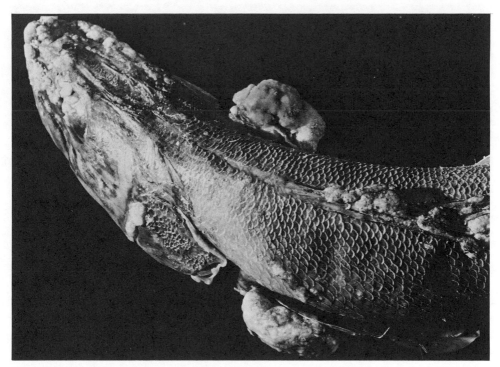

Figure 63   Walleye (fresh water) infected with lymphocystis disease.

although secondary invasion of the wounds by bacteria may cause death. Lymphocystis cells eventually rupture and the skin heals over without scarring. In experimentally induced infections the lesions appeared in 10 to 12 days at 72 to 77 F (22–25 C). The disease may persist for several months or disappear in a few days.

Transmission. The infection is *nonselective;* that is, it does not appear to favor one host over another. It is also highly resistant. Sections of diseased tissue have been known to retain infectivity even after storage at -4 F (-20 C) for two years or after being kept in putrid aquarium water for five days at room temperature. It is also known that wounded fishes are definitely more susceptible to infection, although the virus may gain entrance through the gills of healthy animals. Transmission is effected when the contents of burst cells reach another host or when infected cells are ingested.

Prevention and Treatment. No drugs or other agents are known to cure lymphocystis. Since the disease is contagious, dilution of the water is often helpful. Oxidative chemical filtration techniques may kill free-floating infective cells. Move obviously diseased fishes to different quarters and use the following procedure on the infected tank:

Figure 64   Dorsal fin of a cowfish infected with lymphocystis disease.

HOW TO TREAT LYMPHOCYSTIS

1. Raise the temperature to 77 F (25 C) over a period of two days.
2. Replace 25% of the water daily for two days.
3. Start chemical filtration immediately with ozone or UV irradiation.

10.3   BACTERIA

TUBERCULOSIS

Description. The most prevalent bacterial disease in captive aquarium fishes is tuberculosis. Externally the disease is characterized by discolored patches on the skin. Internally there are yellowish lesions on the organs. When normal functioning of the organs is impaired, the fish dies.

Pathology. The symptoms of fish tuberculosis are slow to appear. At first a fish refuses to eat. It loses weight and spends most of the time hiding in a dark corner with folded fins. Sometimes open sores or ulcers develop on the skin and the fins start to disintegrate. No area of the body—inside or out—may be spared invasion by tubercular bacteria. The liver, intestine, or any other organ may become infected and eventually moribund. In some cases deformation of the bones results in grotesque curvatures of the spine or weird angling of the jaws. Since any of these symptoms may also be characteristic of other bacterial diseases, exact confirmation of fish tuberculosis is impossible without laboratory culture.

Transmission. Transmission in captive fishes is easily made by ingestion of the bacteria with infected food or by direct entry into lesions and open wounds on the body surface. In this latter respect the bacteria would be *secondary invaders*.

Prevention and Treatment. It has been said that tuberculosis is the most common single cause of death among captive fishes. This would seem to preclude any protection by sterilization of the water, especially in small aquariums in which contact is bound to occur anyway. Nevertheless, sterilization with ozone or UV irradiation may prevent the bacteria from reaching overwhelming numbers in times of generally unfavorable conditions.

An even more effective procedure is to remove any specimens with open lesions and isolate them. This prevents transfer of viable bacteria to fishes that are not yet infected.

Any fish that dies of tuberculosis must be removed at once. If others feed on its flesh they, too, will become infected.

VIBRIO DISEASE

Description. "Vibrio disease," caused by bacteria of the genus *Vibrio*, is a common occurrence among aquarium fishes. Many aspects of its natural history and etiology (origin) have not been explained satisfactorily, although the organism has been intensely studied. *Aeromonas*, a closely related form pathogenic in freshwater fishes, produces many of the same symptoms, as does *Pseudomonas*. It is possible, therefore, that many diseases attributed to one of these organisms may actually be caused by another. To complicate matters further some investigators feel that a virus may also be involved. Exact diagnosis is dependent on culturing and identifying the microbe in the laboratory.

Pathology. One of the first signs of vibrio disease is loss of appetite. Infected fishes become inactive and show discolored patches of skin. Later there is a general hemorrhaging of the fins and body surfaces, which then degenerate into ulcerated areas. The anus may be reddened and distended. Another sign is "fin rot," in which one or more of the fins disintegrate. Internally there may be congestion of the liver, kidneys, and intestine.

Transmission. Transmission is from fish to fish or from ingesting the infected flesh of other fishes.

Prevention and Treatment. Vibrio disease reflects the condition of the environment perhaps better than any other disease common to aquarium fishes. Temperature fluctuations, sudden increases in ammonia, inadequate nutrition, overcrowding, and high levels of dissolved organics all contribute to conditions ideal for an outbreak of vibrio disease.

Since *Vibrio* may be a secondary invader, rough handling may be an indirect cause. When fishes are bruised and scratched during capture or transfer, the wounds become open invitations for infection. Loss of scales and mucus sometimes occurs when nets instead of plastic bags are used for capturing. Larger parasites, like worms and crustaceans, leave open sores that also become sites of secondary infection.

Chloramphenicol, or "chloromycetin," is effective against vibrio disease at a concentration of 50 mg/gal (13 mg/liter). Aqueous solutions are stable.

HOW TO TREAT VIBRIO DISEASE

1. Isolate the infected fishes in the treatment tank.
2. Add chloramphenicol in a concentration of 50 mg/gal (13 mg/liter).
3. Leave the fishes in the treatment tank for seven days. During this time, replace 50% of the water daily and renew the solution in the treatment tank with more chloramphenicol to the original concentration.

10.4   FUNGI

ICHTHYOPHONUS HOFERI

Description. There are some 75,000 species of fungi alive in the world today. Many are beneficial, producing our penicillin, bread, beer, and cheese; others are highly pathogenic. Fungi are actually primitive plants with cobweb-like bodies. The body, known as the *thallus*, is composed of filaments radiating out in all directions. Digestive enzymes diffusing from the cells digest the substrate on which the organism is growing—living tissue in the case of *Ichthyophonus hoferi*, the most widespread fungus infectious to fishes.

Typically the fungus may invade and grow in any organ of the body. It reproduces asexually by spore formation (only superficial evidence of the sexual mode of reproduction has been found in *Ichthyophonus*). A mature parasite produces a nearly continuous stream of spores from a structure

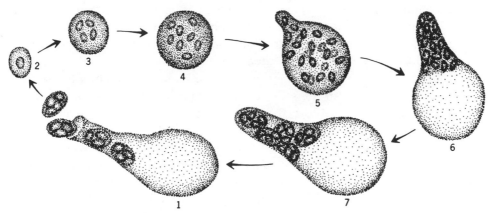

Figure 65   Life history of Ichthyophonus hoferi, *a fungus parasitic in fishes:* (1) *release of spores from a mature hypha;* (2,3,4) *developing thallus;* (5,6,7) *maturing hyphal bodies.*

known as a *hypha* (Figure 65). At maturity the spores escape, enter the bloodstream of the host, and infect other organs of the body. New *hyphal bodies* grow at each site of infection.

Pathology. An infected fish loses weight and skin color. There may be disintegration of the fins in some cases or loss of equilibrium if the parasites have invaded the brain. Sometimes the skin looks rough with yellowish, granular spots deep in the flesh and organs. Death occurs within six months.

Transmission. Ichthyophonus is nonselective and invades a great variety of freshwater and marine fishes, both in temperate and tropical environments. Transmission of spores takes place by direct ingestion, feeding on the flesh of infected fishes, or feeding on small crustaceans that have eaten spores. In the gut of the fish digestive enzymes dissolve the encircling membrane, thus freeing the spores.

Prevention and Treatment. No cure is known. Infected fishes should be removed to another tank immediately. The gravel in the filter bed should be stirred daily and the suspended detritus trapped in the filter fiber of the outside filter. Replace the fiber with new material at least every other day.

10.5 PROTOZOANS

OODINIUM OCELLATUM

Description. The scourge of marine aquariums is *Oodinium ocellatum,* one of the dinoflagellates. The group known as the flagellates (to which dinoflagellates belong) are characterized by a single flagellum, a threadlike extension capable of lashing motions that propel the tiny organism through the water.

Dinoflagellates have modified this arrangement. Besides the flagellum used for swimming, a dinoflagellate has a second one wrapped around its body like a girdle. A fish infected with *Oodinium* loses its irridescent appearance, thereby alluding to the popular name "velvet disease."

The life history of *Oodinium ocellatum* is shown in Figure 66. The parasitic stage is a cyst attached to the gills or skin of its host fish by means of rootlike structures called *rhizoids*. Once it attains a certain size the parasite detaches and sinks to the bottom of the aquarium, imbibing water and increasing in volume by about 25%. The rhizoids are retracted within the cyst and the opening is sealed with a cellulose cap. Shortly thereafter the cellular material recedes from the outer membrane. Now the organism starts to divide internally. Each of the daughter cells it produces in turn divides, and the result is a geometric progression of new cells: first two, then four, then eight, and so forth, until the number reaches 256. This is the *palmella stage*.

The young cells are called *dinospores*. They soon grow their own flagella and break out through the cyst wall to become free-swimming. After awhile they settle to the bottom and secrete cellulose coverings about themselves. After growing the girdle associated with dinoflagellates, along with the typical swimming flagella, a dinospore is ready to find a host fish.

A dinospore has 24 hours to find a host; otherwise it dies. Once attached, the flagella disappear and the parasite grows into a cyst.

Pathology. *Oodinium* seems to prefer the gills (Figure 67), but heavy infections sometimes cover the skin, eyes, and even the inside of the mouth. The adult parasite feeds by extending rhizoids into its host and absorbing living protoplasm. The result is liquifaction of its host's tissues, followed by hemorrhaging and interference with the normal uptake of oxygen across the gill surfaces.

Transmission. Nearly all marine aquarium fishes are subject to infection by *Oodinium*. Massive losses are bound to occur when the parasite is present during periods of general decline in the quality of the water. Poor nutrition is another detrimental factor that can lead to severe *Oodinium* infections. When environmental factors are properly regulated, many fishes are able to build up temporary immunities to *Oodinium* and ward off pathogenic infections. Actual transmission, of course, is from fish to fish. Reinfection is bound to occur within the confines of an aquarium tank.

Prevention and Treatment. From the standpoint of prevention, use of ozone or UV irradiation is said to help control the free-floating stages of *Oodinium*, but this needs to be verified under laboratory conditions. Cupric sulfate ($CuSO_4 \cdot 5H_2O$) is the most commonly used cure. It supposedly kills the dinospores, although this, too, has still to be confirmed experimentally. The cysts are probably impervious or require higher concentrations of copper than most fishes can tolerate. Copper is highly toxic to fishes; it alters proteins within the gills and causes permanent damage, so be sure not to overdose. A level of 0.1 ppm is usually adequate.

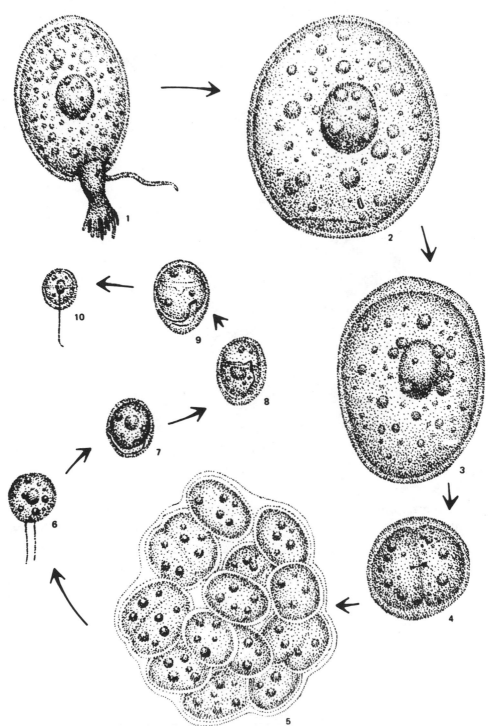

Figure 66 Life history of Oodinium ocellatum, *a parasitic dinoflagellate of marine fishes: (1) cyst, or parasitic stage, showing rhizoids and flagellum (60 x 50 μ); (2) retraction of rhizoids and flagellum and secretion of a cellulose cap; (3) separation of cell material from outer membrane; (4) beginning of cell division, or palmella stage; (5) continuation of cell division (also palmella stage); (6) escaping dinospore; (7,8,9) dinospore with a cellulose covering; (10) mature dinospore ready to attach to a host fish (12 x 8 μ).*

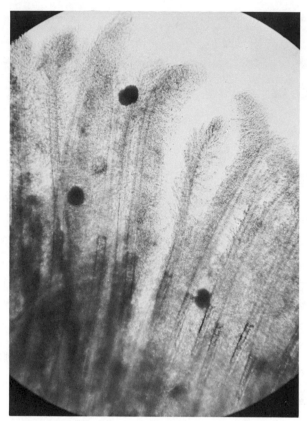

Figure 67   Parasitic stage of Oodinium *attached to the gill filaments of an anemonefish.*

If the treatment tank is small, mix up a stock solution of cupric sulfate to save weighing the amounts of the crystalline form you will need each day.

HOW TO MIX A STOCK COPPER SOLUTION

1. Dissolve 1 g of cupric sulfate ($CuSO_4 \cdot 5H_2O$) in 1 liter of water. One milliliter (ml) of this solution will equal one milligram (mg) of cupric sulfate
2. For a 0.4 ppm cupric sulfate solution (0.1 ppm copper ion) in the treatment tank, add 8 drops (0.4 ml) of stock solution for each liter of water in the tank.

To be successful, copper treatment should be continued for 10 days. The actual amount of copper in solution will decline as it combines with carbonates in the water and precipitates. To sustain a constant level of 0.1 ppm, test the water twice daily with a copper test kit and bring the level back up as necessary.

EXAMPLE.   Water in the treatment tank = 10 gal.

$$10 \times 3.79 = 37.9 \text{ liters.}$$

Using the stock solution,

8 drops/liter = 8×37.9 = 303 drops or 15 ml (20 drops = 1 ml). If after one day the copper ion level in the treatment tank has dropped to 0.05 ppm, add half the original amount of stock solution, which would be 152 drops. You are adding half because the original level has declined by half.

If the cupric sulfate is to be added in its crystalline form instead of in a stock solution, use this formula

$$X = \frac{V \times P \times 3.93}{1000},$$

where X = the weight of the cupric sulfate in grams, V = the volume of the treatment tank in liters, P = ppm copper desired to treat the container, and 3.93 = the amount of cupric sulfate in grams containing one gram of copper ion.

EXAMPLE. V = 200 liters.

P = 0.2 ppm.

$$X = \frac{200 \times 0.2 \times 3.93}{1000},$$

$$X = \frac{157.2}{1000},$$

$$X = 0.16 \text{ g cupric sulfate.}$$

Quinine seems to work well against the dinospore stages of *Oodinium*. Although it is more expensive than copper, it is probably safer. Besides having fewer harmful effects on the fishes, quinine does not kill bacteria, and this means that biological filtration can be sustained throughout treatment. It has been shown experimentally that copper interrupts nitrification in filter beds.

Quinine can be purchased from a druggist. The hydrochloride form is preferable to quinine sulfate because of its greater solubility.

HOW TO TREAT WITH QUININE

1. Add 2 g quinine hydrochloride per 100 liters of water in the treatment tank.
2. Keep the fishes in the solution for a minimum of five days; renew 50% of the water and quinine after the third day.

Figure 68   An angelfish infected with Cryptocaryon irritans.

CRYPTOCARYON IRRITANS

Description. Ciliates are the most highly developed of the protozoans. Most are free-living but many are parasitic. The most common parasitic ciliate infecting marine aquarium fishes is *Cryptocaryon irritans*, the agent that produces the familiar "white-spot disease," or "salt-water ich." The disease is characterized by numerous white nodules about pinhead size on the skin and gills of fishes (Figure 68).

There are three stages in the life cycle of *Cryptocaryon*, as shown in Figure 69. The first stage, called the *trophont*, is the only truly parasitic one. Trophonts are the white spots. The *tomont* stage is next. At some point the trophonts drop off the host fish and enter a reproductive phase. This takes as many as 20 hours at room temperature. Cell division within each tomont is eventually complete and the free-swimming *tomites* (third stage) emerge about the eighth day. Each tomont produces as many as 200 tomites, which then have 24 hours to find a host fish. If they are successful, they burrow into the skin and gills, producing the characteristic white nodules at maturity.

Pathology. The parasites absorb living nutrients, and infections of the gills are especially damaging. Nonselective bacteria are commonly secondary invaders, although the ciliates themselves are the direct cause of death in heavily parasitized fishes.

Transmission. The wide range of host fishes that this organism can infect brands it as a constant menace. Tomites have little difficulty locating suitable hosts within the confining walls of an aquarium. This creates an endless

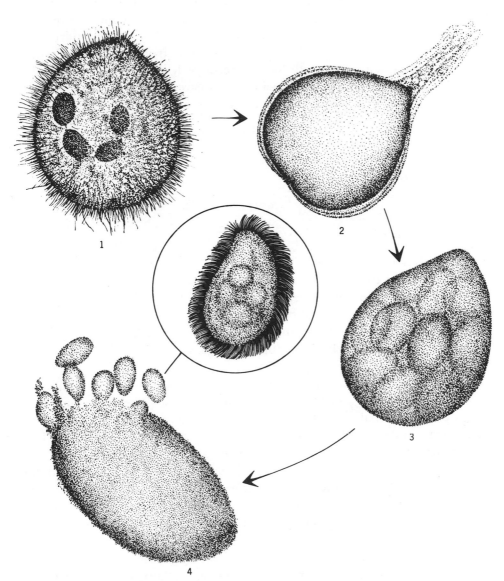

Figure 69 Life history of Cryptocaryon irritans, *a ciliate parasite of marine fishes: (1) trophont, or parasitic stage (to 450 x 350 μ); (2) encysted tomont (shape variable); (3) tomont with developing tomites; (4) free-swimming tomites escaping from ruptured tomont (average 56.5 x 35 μ).*

cycle of infection and reinfection which typically leads to one of two results: ultimate death of all the fishes in the aquarium or an acquired immunity stabilizing at a low-level (latent) infection. The quality of the environment largely dictates the alternative that will win out. If water quality is poor, nutrition inadequate, and conditions overcrowded, the animals stand only a limited chance of survival. They will have no resistance to sustain an immunity, and thus will allow the latent infection to become pathogenic.

Prevention and Treatment. Same as for *Oodinium ocellatum.*

10.6 FLATWORMS

BENEDENIA MELLENI

Description. Historically it would seem a worm is ". . . any elongated creeping thing that is not obviously something else." So said two noted parasitologists. From the time of the ancient Greeks until quite recently it was thought that worms were generated spontaneously from mud, manure, ooze, or any other repugnant substance. It was also believed that the parasitic forms originated in excessive moisture or putrefying matter. To the bewildered aquarist such ideas may not seem farfetched during times of sudden infestation in his aquarium.

There are three classes of flatworms which, speaking in evolutionary terms, are the lowliest worms of all. Two are parasitic. The class Turbellaria is composed of small, unassuming creatures content to spend their lives as free-living members of the aquatic community. The class Cestoda constitutes the tapeworms, a large and highly specialized group of parasites. Our concern here is the class Trematoda, or the *flukes*, as they are commonly called. The name "fluke" has an interesting history. Sometime in the seventeenth century it was postulated that certain parasitic worms were landlocked leeches or even fishes. The term fluke has its derivation in the Anglo-Saxon *floc*, meaning flounder.

Many parasites (e.g., the tapeworms) require an intermediate host before they can complete their life histories, as explained in the opening of this chapter. For such an organism an aquarium fish may simply be a step along the way. The final host may be a gull, a seal, or even a bigger fish. There are two major orders of flukes: Monogenea and Digenea. The digenetic flukes all require at least one intermediate host. The adult form is an internal parasite and cannot be seen. Digenetic flukes are of little concern to the aquarist. The monogenetic flukes, on the other hand, can be quite important. These worms develop directly. As a result, the monogenetic flukes can potentially take over an aquarium.

I always find it fascinating to review the characteristics of flatworms. It's amazing that such successful and widespread creatures can exist at all, considering their sparse anatomy. The typical flatworm has only a rudimentary digestive system (a mouth but not an anus). It has no body cavity, no skeletal structure, no circulatory system, and no means of respiration. It has become so highly specialized that it relies on its host to carry out these functions. What flukes can do by themselves, however, they do without equal—and that is to reproduce. A mature fluke is a living egg machine.

One of the most troublesome flukes is *Benedenia melleni* (formerly called *Epibdella melleni*), a small monogenetic fluke that infests the skin, eyes, nasal passages, and gill cavities of a great variety of marine fishes (serranids, surgeons, triggers, and wrasses, to name a few). The larval and adult stages of this organism are illustrated in Figure 70. For all practical purposes we

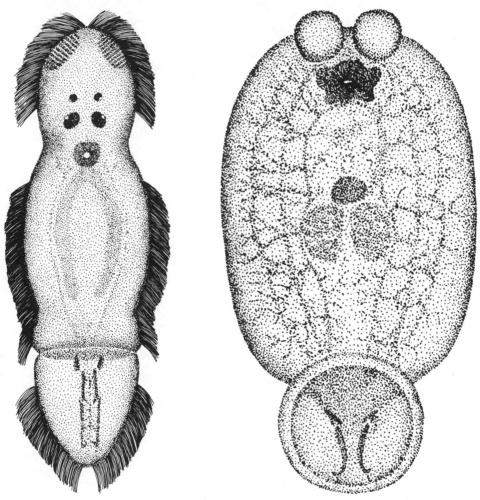

Figure 70   The parasitic fish fluke, Benedenia melleni: *larval stage* (left) *shortly after hatching* (225 μ); *the adult form* (right), *which reaches a length of 4 mm.*

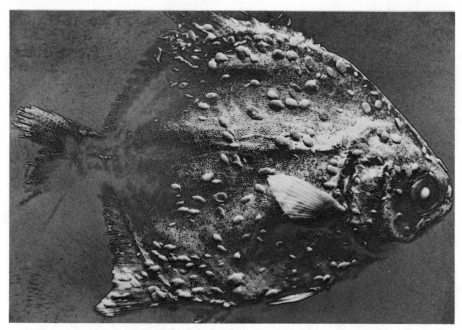

Figure 71   Juvenile pompano heavily infested with Benedenia melleni.

can call *Benedenia* nonselective. The parasite was thought to have been a West Indian form when it was discovered by scientists at the New York Aquarium in 1927. We now know that it readily attaches to fishes from the Mediterranean, Indo-Pacific, or anywhere else.

Benedenia lays its eggs directly on its host. In aquariums kept at room temperature the eggs hatch in five to eight days. The larvae are ciliated and swim for six hours. If no host can be found, they sink to the bottom and crawl feebly about for awhile, then die. If a host is located, the larvae lose their cilia and become actively parasitic, feeding on the mucus and blood of their victim.

Pathology. Severe infestations can cause loss of scales, even to the point of exposing underlying muscle tissue. The open wounds are ripe for secondary invasion by bacteria. A heavily infested fish is shown in Figure 71.

Transmission. Larval forms attach directly to host fishes.

Prevention and Treatment. A quarantine period of two weeks is mandatory for all new fishes. This localizes any outbreak of the parasites. Each tank should have its own cleaning utensils, since larvae can be transferred from tank to tank on a net or sponge. Obviously infested fishes should be removed at once to a separate tank to keep down the transfer of parasites to uninfested fishes.

A dip in fresh water for 15 minutes, or until the parasites drop off, is the best treatment for *Benedenia melleni*, and also the safest for the host fishes.

10.7   CRUSTACEANS

FISH LICE

Description. Argulida (members of the genus *Argulus*), or "fish lice," are large external parasites that often reach several millimeters in length. They have a flattened carapace, or body shell, and the basal portion of the first antennae is modified into a claw. Parts of the mouth have evolved into sucking disks. Fish lice are highly mobile and are often seen running nimbly over the surfaces of their hosts. A typical representative of the group is the one in Figure 72.

Mature parasites leave the host fish and lay as many as 250 eggs on some fixed object in the tank. The egg masses are large enough to be seen with the naked eye. After hatching the young develop directly, going through six larval stages before becoming parasitic adults after the seventh molt.

Pathology. The mandibles are shaped like a sting and are associated with a venom gland. The tubular mouth is inserted into the wound opened by the jaws, and blood and mucus of the host are sucked out. The sting of fish lice

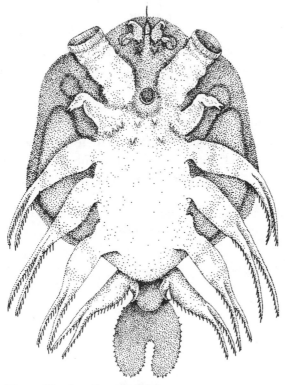

Figure 72   Argulus *the fish louse.*

is toxic and is often enough by itself to kill smaller fishes. The poison is known to cause degeneration of cells in areas beneath the skin. In addition, the open wounds made by fish lice are potential sites of secondary invasion by bacteria.

Transmission. Transmission is direct. Within the close confines of an aquarium a fish louse can leave one victim and easily attach to another. In like manner the young have no trouble finding hosts.

Prevention and Treatment. Fish lice are incredibly durable, and no successful treatment that does not also injure the host has yet been found. Host fishes should be captured and their parasites removed with tweezers.

The best prevention is to quarantine new specimens for two weeks before placing them in established aquariums. Again, be sure that each tank has its own cleaning utensils. Complete sterilization of the tank and cleaning utensils (see Section 10.8) is the only means of eradicating fish lice once they have gained control.

10.8 STERILIZATION

There are occasions when a tank must be completely sterilized. This is the most serious event possible in aquarium keeping because it means upsetting the careful biological balance within the system simply to kill one trouble-some group of organisms. At such times it would be wise to review your entire operational procedure and try to determine where you went wrong. Make no mistake about it: when conditions reach a rock-bottom low that necessitates sterilizing the tank, it is usually your own fault. Disease organisms were either transferred to a healthy aquarium on your hands or cleaning utensils or by an infected animal that somehow slipped through quarantine undetected. It may also be that you failed to test the water routinely and take stock of chemical changes that lowered the disease resistance of your specimens. Wherever the fault lies you must recognize it and prevent it from happening again.

There is never any need to tear down a tank simply to sterilize it. This can be done by recycling a strong oxidative substance through the filter bed and tank water.

HOW TO STERILIZE AN AQUARIUM TANK

1. Remove those specimens that are still living and put them in treatment tanks. Remove fiberglass tank decorations and soak them in a bucket of fresh water for the duration of the treatment period. Natural corals, rocks, and gravel should remain in the aquarium tank.
2. Fill the tank to the very top. Tap water is good enough.
3. Put all cleaning utensils into the tank (sponges, siphon hoses, nets, etc.).
4. Add $\frac{1}{2}$ oz of a liquid chlorine bleach per gallon of water.
5. Let the solution circulate for 24 hours.
6. Add $\frac{1}{2}$ oz of granular sodium thiosulfate for every 10 gallons of water to neutralize the chlorine.
7. Let the water circulate for two hours.
8. Siphon out all the water and throw it away.
9. Rinse the gravel and tank with several changes of tap water.
10. Refill the tank to the very top with tap water.
11. Let the water circulate for eight hours; then remove the cleaning utensils.
12. Empty the tank, refill it with new sea water, and start the conditioning process over again (see Chapter 3, Section 1).
13. When you add new animals, be sure they have been quarantined and show no signs of pathogenic infections or infestations.

10.9 NONINFECTIOUS DISEASES

GAS-BUBBLE DISEASE

Description. The most common noninfectious malady to afflict aquarium fishes is "gas-bubble disease," or *exophthalmus*, which appears suddenly as air bubbles underneath the skin and eye membranes (Figure 73). The origin of this condition is seldom biological. Most often it results from an excess of dissolved gases in water, a condition known as *supersaturation*. Water can become supersaturated by gases (notably nigrogen gas, N_2, but occasionally oxygen) when they are forced into solution under pressure.

Pathology. Gas bubbles may form on all external surfaces, the lining of the body cavity, and even inside the mouth. The surface tissue of the gills becomes swollen and is eventually destroyed, making respiration difficult. In many cases the red blood cells throughout the circulatory system rupture. Inside the mouth there is excessive tissue degeneration. Muscle and kidney tissue is greatly altered or destroyed, and the liver cells may become distended beyond recognition.

Transmission. There is no transmission since the condition is not infectious. All fishes in an aquarium are equally subject to gas-bubble disease when conditions are right, although some species are prone to develop the condition more than others.

Figure 73   A chinook salmon fingerling with gas-bubble disease.

Prevention and Treatment. In the aquarium, power filters are usually the cause of gas-bubble disease. If there is an air leak on the suction side of the filter unit (which draws the water from the tank into the filter), the minute amount of air entering through a loose connection or faulty seal in the pump can be forced back into the tank under pressure. If the pump is the source, the condition is called *cavitation*, the process by which gases are driven into the water under pressure by mechanical forces.

Power filters are dangerous and unnecessary. As the pumps become worn with use, they pose a constant threat of cavitating and causing supersaturation of the water with nitrogen gas. If such units are used, the discharge should be aimed horizontally across the surface of the water. Never leave the discharge tube from a power filter completely submerged or let the effluent water be driven vertically into the tank.

Nothing can be done for animals afflicted with gas-bubble disease. Insofar as the water is concerned, aeration is the only means of correcting the situation. Simply let the airlifts from the subgravel filter do their work. Eventually the excess gas will be driven back into the atmosphere.

The Art

Chapter Eleven

≋≋≋≋≋

Decorating

11.1 THEME

Not long ago a fashionable aquarium was one in which the gravel was dyed brilliant colors. Little treasure chests were in vogue, perhaps flanked by a plastic octopus or two with bubbles rising from the tops of their heads. In the center stood the inevitable diver, knee-deep in marbles and looking out at you with a blank, ceramic expression.

Fortunately this practice is dying out and is being replaced by a feeling of greater awareness. In the old days no one could be faulted for paying so little attention to the natural environments of their animals; after all, only a handful of people had ever seen the bottom of the ocean.

But the uninformed no longer have an excuse. The development of the aqualung has made the bottom of the sea accessible to anyone in reasonably good health. Even the armchair oceanographer can educate himself simply by watching television, going to films, and reading contemporary newspapers, magazines, and books. Nature, of course, can never be duplicated perfectly, but trying and partly succeeding is one of the more satisfying aspects of aquarium keeping.

Many people have been to a public aquarium. The size and diversity of the exhibits can be breathtaking, but what makes them truly impressive is the great pains taken by their curators to simulate the different habitats of the animals. A coral reef contains only coral-reef fishes, and creatures of the North Pacific tidepools are shown in surroundings of dark and jagged basalt. Professional aquarists realize that the animals make up a very important part of the exhibit but that the decorations are important too. When the right combination of animals and tank decorations is used, the end result is a stunning rendition of nature.

The same principles pertain to decorating the home aquarium. If you are keeping coral-reef fishes, every effort should be made to supply the aquarium with corals. If your animals have been captured along the New England coast, pick up a boxful of pink beach granite and local shells and use them as decor. The use of natural materials will put your animals into proper perspective. When approached thoughtfully, decorating the aquarium can be a means of creative expression. With practice you will learn to achieve that rare balance of scientific accuracy and pleasing aesthetics.

11.2 MATERIALS AND THEIR PREPARATION

Some natural materials are unsuited to a captive environment. As we have just seen, the objects you add to your aquarium should be pertinent to the theme of the exhibit and pleasing to look at, but they must also be chemically safe and fairly durable.

CORALS

Selection. Many corals are too delicate for use in the home aquarium; some, in fact, seem to break apart when touched. To use them is obviously impractical. Others are finely branched or contain deep convolutions and crevices that trap bits of uneaten food and other debris, thus adding to the general pollution of the water. Pipe organ coral is typical of this last group (Figure 74). It is perfectly suitable for decorating a dry diorama (see Section 4) but should not be immersed directly in the aquarium.

On the other hand, the heavy rounded species shown in Figures 75, 76, and 77 are excellent either in the aquarium itself or in the dry diorama.

Figure 74   Pipe organ coral.

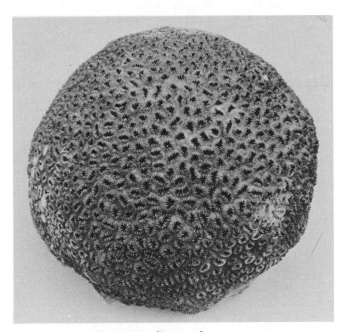

Figure 75   Star coral.

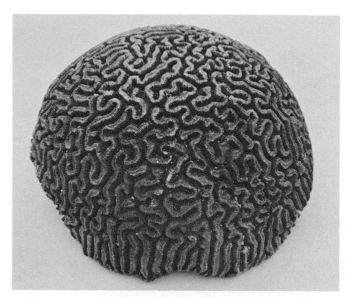

Figure 76   Brain coral.

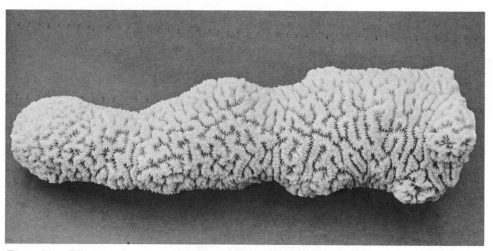

Figure 77   Pillar coral.

Cleaning. Corals taken directly from the ocean must be cleaned before they are safe to use in the aquarium. The coral head you buy in a store is the bleached stony skeleton of a colony of animals. Your newly collected corals must be made to look the same. If the remains of the coral animals (called *polyps*) are not removed, they will quickly pollute the aquarium water.

HOW TO CLEAN NEWLY COLLECTED CORAL

1. Place newly collected corals outdoors in the sun and let them weather for two weeks. After this time check to see if most of the organic covering has come off. Weathered corals may still contain some organic matter, but it should be loose and easy to remove.
2. Wash off each piece of coral with a garden hose.
3. Place the corals in a plastic container, such as a bucket or dishpan, and cover them completely with a solution of one part liquid chlorine bleach and three parts water. Let them soak for three days.
4. Pour off the old solution and renew it. Let the corals soak for another three days.
5. The corals are now bleached white but the remaining chlorine needs to be removed or it will poison your aquarium animals. Soak the corals in clean tap water for three days, changing the water at least twice daily. If after three days even the faintest odor of chlorine persists, soak them until it disappears completely.

STONES

Selection. Beach stones, or stones from intertidal areas, are best because they have already weathered for a long time in sea water. Be careful that those you pick do not come from anywhere near a sewage outfall or factory effluent.

Cleaning. Scrub the stones thoroughly with a stiff brush and hot tap water.

WOOD

Selection. Choose driftwood that is well weathered and no longer contains cell sap or resins. The wood must not be rotten or it will crumble in the aquarium and become difficult to remove. Again be careful that the material has not soaked up water from a nearby source of pollution.

Cleaning. Scrub the wood with a stiff brush and hot tap water; then soak it for a week in tap water, changing the water twice daily during this period.

11.3 FIBERGLASS DECORATIONS

Several public aquariums have developed procedures for making artificial decorations out of fiberglass. These have distinct advantages. After cleaning and bleaching, a natural coral formation is white and sterile looking, devoid of the delicate, living colors it once had. Natural corals are also fragile and easily broken, as well as heavy and expensive to ship, and they become more and more fragile the older they get. Moreover, a suitable piece of cured coral fetches an exorbitant price, especially from the inland hobbyist.

Artificial corals are the opposite. They are durable and lightweight and can be fabricated cheaply in their natural colors. The process described here involves molding. Once the mold for a particular piece is made, you can manufacture any number of duplicates. All you need is the original coral head from which to take a mold.

SELECTING THE PROPER CORALS

I shall use a coral head for illustrative purposes, although you can just as easily make artificial sandstone, granite, shale, logs, or even brick walls.

The proper corals for molding can have extensive *surface relief* (texture, pockmarks and shallow ridges, protuberances, and crevices), but they cannot be thin or branched. A quick glance at Figure 78 illustrates the point. The coral head at the top is basically round and compact in shape, a perfect piece to be duplicated in fiberglass. The coral at the bottom is a piece of staghorn coral. It is thin and delicately branched and would be very difficult to reproduce by the process about to be described. A rule of thumb is that anything from which a flexible rubber mold can be peeled can be reproduced in fiberglass by using the process given here. The three best corals to work with are the brain, pillar, and star corals already shown in preceding illustrations.

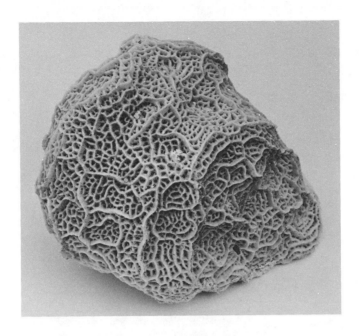

*Figure 78   The coral head at the top has a shape suitable for reproduction in fiberglass·
The coral formation at the bottom is too branched.*

MATERIALS

A complete list of materials is given in Table 13. Their functions are discussed in this section.

Table 13   Fiberglassing Supplies

Liquid latex rubber (1 gal)
Polyester resin (2 gal)
Acetone (1 qt)
Brushes:
   Artist's no. 8 (2)
   One-inch natural bristle (6)
Pigments:
   Black (4 oz)
   White (8 oz)
   Chocolate brown (4 oz)
   Yellow (8 oz)
   Dark green (4 oz)
Plastic spoons (12)
Silicone spray (two 16-oz cans)
Thickener (1 lb)
Modeling clay (1 lb)
Hardener ($\frac{1}{2}$ pt)
Metal measuring spoons (1 set)
Plastic safety goggles (1 pair)
Rubber or disposable plastic gloves
Tin cans (12)
Stirring sticks

Latex Molding Rubber. The latex rubber suitable for molding comes as a thick liquid and is applied at full strength to the original coral head with a paint brush. It if becomes necessary to thin the rubber, use a solution of two teaspoons of concentrated ammonia in a pint of water. Concentrated ammonia is available at most drugstores. Liquid rubber can be purchased at hobby shops.

Polyester Resin. Sometimes this resin is called fiberglass or fiberglass resin. Many types are available, but the best to use for this purpose are the thicker, low-cobalt resins designed for coating and not for casting. Generally, they are inexpensive (about $5/gal) and can take up to 15% by volume of added pigment. Since the pigments are difficult to measure accurately, it is better to be safe and choose a resin in which the quantity isn't critical. Resins used to build and repair fiberglass boats are suitable. They have been manufactured to resist water spotting and will also take large amounts of pigment. The technical salesman at a chemical supply house dealing with resins can recommend a brand. Check the yellow pages in the telephone directory under "Resins" or "Fiberglass."

Acetone. Acetone is used to clean brushes after they have been immersed in resin. Use this solvent to clean your hands and to wipe up resin spills. Ideally, you should wear rubber or disposable plastic gloves when working with resins and acetone, for both have a drying effect on the skin. If gloves are not available, wash your hands thoroughly and use a moistening cream.

Brushes. Brushes are used to apply the liquid latex to the coral and also to apply the resin to the mold. Do not use brushes with nylon bristles, particularly in the resin. These bristles have a tendency to pull out and remain stuck to the object you are making.

For applying latex rubber use a 1- or 2-in. brush. Squeeze out the remaining latex after each use and leave the brush soaking in a can of soapy water. When you are ready to use the brush again, simply squeeze out the water and shake it dry. Rubber that dries on the bristles can be removed with a wire brush.

For applying the first coat of resin to the mold, an artist's brush (No. 8, short-bristle) is the best. The subsequent coats of resin can be applied with a 1-in. brush. The brushes should be cleaned in acetone immediately after use, then shaken dry.

Pigments. The color of your fiberglass decorations is blended into the resin, not painted on afterward. This makes it permanent and non-fading. The pigments you select should be manufactured for use with polyester resins. They are generally sold as pastes or liquids; liquids are preferable. The five basic colors are black, white, yellow, chocolate brown, and dark green. Use a different plastic spoon with each pigment and keep the spoon in a separate tin can. The pigments are messy, and I have found this procedure as satisfactory as any. The excess pigment simply drips from the spoon into the can. Resin and pigments can usually be bought from the same dealer.

Silicone Spray. Used as a mold release, silicone acts as an inert lubricant and enables you to peel the mold from the coral. Without it the mold sometimes rips, leaving bits of rubber sticking to the coral. Any of the silicone sprays made for home or automotive use are suitable.

Thickener. Thickener is composed of fumed silica or asbestos. Most chemical supply houses and hobby shops that carry resins also handle resin thickeners. The thickener alters the consistency of the resin without changing its color or other properties, much as flour thickens gravy without changing its flavor.

Modeling Clay. Modeling clay is used to fill deep holes and crevices in the original coral. These places, unless filled, make it difficult to peel off the mold.

Hardener. The resin hardener is sometimes referred to as the "catalyst."

Without it the resin will remain a liquid indefinitely. Unpigmented resins need an average of one-quarter ounce of hardener per quart and have a drying time of 30 to 45 minutes. Adding pigments prolongs the drying time 15 minutes or so. Polyester resins dry, or "cure," by heat. The hardener reacts with the cobalt in the resin and raises the temperature. Preparing the materials in direct sunlight may accelerate the curing time because the added heat will augment that produced by the action of the hardener.

Safety Goggles. There is always the possibility that resin may splash in your eyes. Goggles will prevent this, but in case it does happen wash your eyes immediately with lots of cold water and then see a doctor at once.

Kitchen Measuring Spoons. A set of kitchen measuring spoons is useful for measuring quantities of hardener. The more hardener added to a batch of resin, the quicker the curing time. Experiment with different amounts of hardener until you arrive at a curing time that is convenient.

Other Materials. Clean tin cans from the kitchen are ideal for mixing small batches of resin.

One final but important note before describing the actual procedures: fiberglassing is a toxic process. It should never be carried out in a room with inadequate ventilation. A covered porch or open garage is ideal.

THE MOLD

The preparation of the mold is the first in a series of important steps. Keep the container of liquid rubber tightly sealed between applications or the material will dry and become useless. Above all, remember that it contains ammonia and should *never* be applied near an aquarium tank containing living animals.

HOW TO MAKE RUBBER MOLDS

1. Select a clean piece of coral. No dead tissue, algae, or other debris of any sort should be stuck to it. The latex will reproduce every bit of the surface of the coral in exact detail, including the dirty areas.
2. Check for deep holes or crevices in the coral. If you find any, fill them with modeling clay, as shown in Figure 79.
3. Spray the coral head lightly with silicone but make sure to cover every bit of the surface, as shown in Figure 80.
4. Apply the first coat of liquid rubber with a paint brush (Figure 81). The first coat is the most critical, since it will duplicate the surface relief of the coral (Figure 82). Use the brush with a dabbing motion to force rubber into every depression. Allow a full 24 hours for the first coat to dry. Subsequent coats take less time.
5. Brush on another coat after 24 hours, again using the dabbing motion.
6. Apply at least six coats of rubber in all. If the mold is to be used several times, 8 to 10 coats are recommended.
7. When the last coat has dried, peel off the mold. Start by freeing all edges, as shown in Figure 83; then work it evenly all around. The last part to be peeled should be the very top. If you now examine the mold, you will see that the surface relief of the coral head has been reproduced precisely in latex (Figure 84).

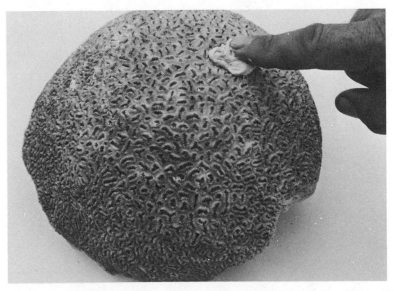

Figure 79   The first step in making a rubber mold is to fill the deep holes with modeling clay.

Figure 80   Spray the coral head lightly with silicone spray.

Figure 81   Apply the liquid rubber with a paint brush. Be sure to fill in all the surface relief.

Figure 82 Closeup photograph of a head of star coral showing the intricate pattern. This detail must be duplicated in the rubber mold.

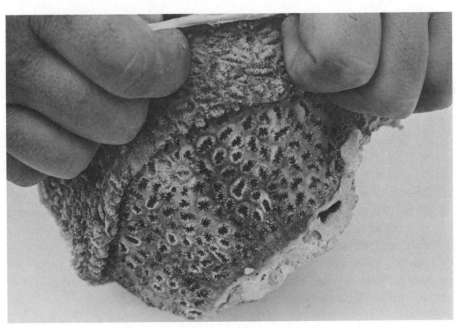

Figure 83 To peel the mold from the coral, start by freeing the edges all around.

Figure 84   Closeup photograph of the mold showing how the detail in the coral has been reproduced.

APPLYING THE RESIN

The first two coats of resin applied to the inside of the mold are called *color coats* because they contain pigment. Subsequent coats can be colorless, since only the first two will be visible.

Most living corals are different shades of brown and it is advisable to study carefully as many color photographs of coral as you can. The actual skill involved in this process is in the application of color. Examine the inside of the mold and also the piece of coral from which it was made. You can see that the high points on the inside of the mold actually are crevices in the piece of coral. Conversely, depressions on the mold are the high spots on the coral. It is critical to remember this fact, because if you don't the application of colors may come out reversed.

You will be painting the inside of the mold with a brush, and therefore the first coat of resin applied will actually be the surface of the finished piece of fiberglass coral. Remember that you will be stripping the rubber away eventually and that the first coat of resin—not the last —will be what meets the eye.

HOW TO APPLY THE FIRST COLOR COAT

1. Pour a small amount of resin into one of the cans.
2. Add thickener until it takes on a consistency of molasses.
3. Add the pigments. Mixing colors can be done skillfully only with practice. To color the resin take a tiny bit of pigment on the end of a plastic spoon and let it drip slowly into the can. At the same time stir the resin, as shown in Figure 85. Stop adding pigment when the resin becomes fully colored. Since you are probably not measuring your pigment, do not add too much or you will pass the recommended maximum of 15%. Pigments of different colors can be mixed together in the resin so long as the total quantity does not exceed the maximum level.
4. Turn the mold inside out and spray it lightly with silicone, as shown in Figure 86.
5. Add the hardener to the resin and stir until it is mixed thoroughly (Figure 87).
6. With the small brush (No. 8) apply the resin to the high points of the mold only (Figure 88). Be careful not to let the resin drip into the crevices of the mold. If it does, then it is too thin. Stop and add more thickener (Figure 89).
7. Turn the mold right-side out again before the resin hardens.
8. Clean the brush in acetone immediately. Let the mold cure overnight.

Figure 85   Blend the color pigments into the resin by dripping small amounts into the mixing can with a plastic spoon and stirring it at the same time.

153

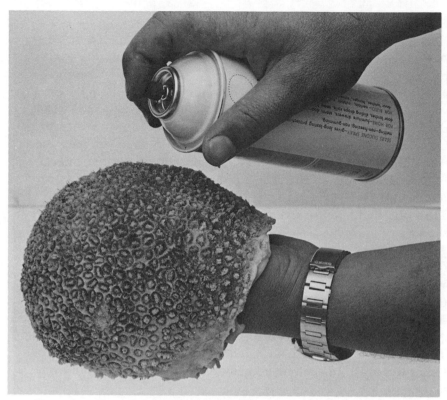

Figure 86   Turn the mold inside-out and spray it lightly with silicone spray.

Figure 87   Add the hardener and stir the resin until it is thoroughly mixed.

154

Figure 88   When painting on the first color coat, apply the resin (mixed to the consistency of molasses) to the high points of the mold only. These will become the low spots on the finished piece.

Figure 89   Add thickener until the resin is the right consistency. This must be done for all coats, from first to last.

HOW TO APPLY THE SECOND COLOR COAT

1. The second color coat can be added as soon as the first coat dries. Mix it the same way, only slightly thinner and lighter in color. If the first coat was dark brown, for example, the second should be similar but with more yellow or white pigment to lighten it. It should be thinner because this time you *want* it to run into the crevices.
2. Do not turn the mold inside-out. Using the 1-in. brush, paint the entire inside of the mold with the second color coat. No part of the latex should be left uncovered nor should there be any of the first coat left unpainted, as shown in Figure 90.
3. Clean the brush immediately in acetone. Let the mold cure overnight.

Figure 90   No part of the mold should be left uncovered after the second color coat has been applied. The second coat should be a little lighter in color than the first.

FINISHING COATS

When you paint a wall, the finishing coats are the last to be applied and the ones you see when the job is finished. The opposite is true of molding. Here the first coats applied are the ones you see, and the finishing coats are the undercoats added merely to give the end product a solid base.

HOW TO APPLY THE FINISHING COATS

1. Mix a batch of resin to the thickness of molasses; then color it black. The coloration gives a solid backing to any spots in the first coats that may be thin and slightly translucent.
2. Most pieces should have at least two more finishing coats (three in all), which should be mixed thicker than molasses— almost like putty—and can be any color or colorless. Concentrate on building up the edges of the piece where it is most likely to break.
3. Let the piece cure overnight between coats.

FINAL CURE

After the last coat has dried the mold must be peeled off. Peel it the same way you peeled the original coral; work all the edges free first or you will tear the rubber.

It should be clear by now that the first coats of resin are the ones that show. The first color coat, which was painted over a high spot on the mold, becomes the low spot on the end-product once the mold has been stripped away.

The finished piece, as it now stands, may be toxic to the animals in your aquarium. Pigments in particular are poisonous, and if any are directly exposed to the water and not completely mixed with the resin they could gradually leach out. This is the reason for the final cure.

HOW TO MAKE THE FINAL CURE

1. Allow the piece to dry in the air for at least a week. It is best to leave it in the sun. Rain, of course, won't hurt it.
2. After a week, cook it in your oven for 8 hours at 115 F (46 C).
3. At the end of this time the resin smell should have disappeared. If it lingers, leave the piece in the oven for another 8 hours or until all traces of odor are gone.

A sample piece, along with the original coral from which the mold was taken, is shown in Figure 91.

Figure 91   A piece of real star coral (right) *and its fiberglass duplicate cast in living color* (left).

11.4   THE DRY DIORAMA

The *diorama* is simply a dry compartment pushed against the back of the aquarium tank. It contains the same kind of gravel as the aquarium and is decorated in the same theme. The purpose is to make the display look bigger than it really is. A typical diorama exhibit is shown in Figure 92.

Few curators of public aquariums are ever certain just how people evaluate their displays. Surveys are helpful, although they always seem contrived, at least to me, and not spontaneous enough to be completely honest. Occasionally a visitor approaches a curator with such a different point of view that he lays to rest once and for all the question of whether the exhibits have succeeded or failed. Such moments are worth a thousand surveys.

Something like this happened to me a few years ago. The Aquarium of Niagara Falls had been open for only two months, and the curatorial personnel were still actively building and changing exhibits. Several exhibits had dioramas, but we weren't sure how they were being received. Was the public fooled into thinking the displays were twice as deep as they really were? No one knew.

I was working in the laboratory late one night when I noticed a jaunty little man in a mild state of intoxication. He was studying each display closely, even bending down and peering up at the corners. Before heading for the exit he knocked on my door.

HOW TO MAKE AND DECORATE A DRY DIORAMA

1. Cut a piece of half-inch plywood the same size as the top of the tank.
2. Cut off the corners of one side until the wood takes the shape of a flattened semicircle (Figure 93).
3. Bend a piece of masonite or sheet metal around the plywood to form the back. Be sure it is slightly taller than the tank or you will be able to see over the top of the diorama when looking into the front of the aquarium.
4. Do not cut the material until you have determined the correct height by observation. After cutting it, nail it to the plywood.
5. Spray the back with light or dark blue enamel. Flat paints look better than those that dry semiglossy or glossy (Figure 94).
6. Set the diorama in place and cover the plywood bottom with gravel to the same depth as in the aquarium. Be sure the layers of gravel are even inside and out; the visual transition from aquarium to diorama is ineffective if the height of the gravel is greater in one than in the other.
7. Decorate the diorama. Corals with deep crevices can be used here, since they are not in contact with the water.
8. Arrange the lighting so that the diorama receives some of it. Ideally, a well-lighted aquarium is brightest in front and gets darker (or fades away) near the back. This takes the emphasis off the back and magnifies the illusion of greater depth.

"I want to congratulate you guys," he said in a slightly slurred voice, "on what fine displays you have."

"Thank you," I replied, proud that someone had noticed our efforts.

"One thing bothers me," he continued. "I've been to aquariums all over the world, but I've never seen aquatic mice before. Where d'you get 'em?"

The question puzzled me and I asked him to be more specific.

"I'll show you," he said, and led the way to one of the 200-gallon displays with a South Pacific theme. Sure enough, climbing out of a large basket sponge was a little brown mouse. It gave us a furtive glance, then scurried across the floor of the tank and disappeared under a ledge of coral.

The man studied the spot where the mouse had been. Finally he looked at me and muttered, "That's the best display I ever saw."

The exhibit was a complete success. The mouse, of course, had been living in the diorama!

Figure 92   Aquarium with a diorama.

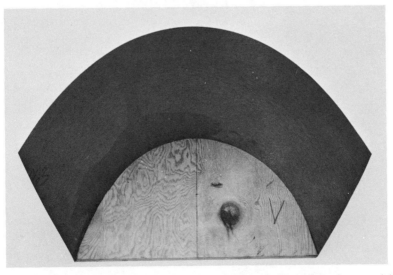

Figure 93   The bottom of the diorama should be a piece of plywood cut in a semicircle. The flat side is the same length as the aquarium tank. The back is a piece of masonite.

161

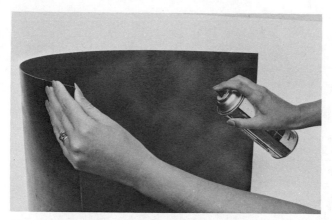

Figure 94   Spray the inside of the diorama with a flat paint. Blue looks best.

Credits for Illustrations

The pen and ink drawings are the work of Frances McKittrick Watkins. Unless stated otherwise, all graphs, photographs, and tables are my own original work.

Table 1	Todd, The Water Encyclopedia, Water Information Center, copyright 1970.
Table 2	Adapted from Spotte (1970).
Figure 4	Aquarium Systems, Inc.
Table 3	Adapted from Gosner (1971).
Figure 8	Aquarium Systems, Inc.
Figure 11	Metaframe Corporation.
Figure 14	Eugene G. Danner Mfg. Inc.
Figure 16	Redrawn after Spotte (1970).
Figure 17	Eugene G. Danner Mfg. Inc.
Tables 4–5	Various sources.
Figure 21	From Spotte (1970).
Table 6	Adapted from Gosner (1971).
Figures 23–27	Redrawn by courtesy of George Tchobanoglous.
Figures 28–30	From Spotte (1970).
Figure 32	Redrawn by permission of Sidney Ellner, Ultraviolet Purification Systems, Inc.
Table 7	Adapted by permission of Sidney Ellner, Ultraviolet Purification Systems, Inc.
Table 8	Reprinted by permission of the Journal of the Fisheries Research Board of Canada.
Table 9	Adapted from Spotte (1970).
Figure 39	Redrawn after Marler and Hamilton (1966).
Figure 41	Drawn from a photograph by Lennart Nilsson in THE SEA (1961), Time, Inc.
Figure 42	Drawn from a photograph by Charles Walcott in Burnett (1961), American Museum of Natural History.
Figure 43	Drawn from a photograph by Carleton Ray in WONDROUS WORLD OF FISHES (1965), National Geographic Society.
Figure 45	Drawn from a photograph by Harry Pederson in THE SEA (1961), Time, Inc.
Table 12	Adapted from Peterson and Robinson (1967).

Figures 55,
  62–64, 67,
  and 71   Osborn Laboratories of Marine Science, New York Zoological Society.
Figure 65   Redrawn after Wolf and Wolf (1949).
Figure 66   Redrawn after Nigrelli (1936).
Figure 69   Redrawn after Nigrelli and Ruggieri (1966).
Figure 70   Redrawn after Jahn and Kuhn (1932).
Figure 72   Redrawn after various sources.
Figure 73   Western Fish Disease Laboratory, U. S. Department of the Interior.

References

~~~~~~~~

ALLEN, G. R.

    1971   Anemonefishes. TFH Publications (Jersey City). 288 pp.

ANDERSON, J. I. W., and D. A. CONROY

    1970   Vibrio diseases in marine fishes. *In* A Symposium on Diseases of Fishes and Shellfishes. Amer. Fish. Soc. Spec. Publ. No. 5 (Washington). 526 pp.

ATZ, J. W., AND D. FAULKNER

    1971   Aquarium Fishes. Viking Press (New York). 112 pp.

BOHLKE, J. E., and C. C. G. CHAPLIN

    1968   Fishes of the Bahamas and Adjacent Tropical Waters. The Academy of Natural Sciences of Philadelphia (Philadelphia). 771 pp.

BUCHSBAUM, R., and L. J. MILNE

    1960   The Lower Animals: Living Invertebrates of the World. Doubleday (New York). 303 pp.

BURNETT, A. L.

    1961   Enigma of an echinoderm. *Nat. Hist.*, **70**:10–19.

CONROY, D. A.

    1968   Partial bibliography on the bacterial diseases of fish: an annotated bibliography for the years 1870–1966. FAO Fisheries Technical Paper No. 73 (Rome). 75 pp.

CROSS, D. G.

    1972   A review of methods to control ichthyophthiriasis. *Prog. Fish-Cult.*, **34**:165–170.

ELIASSEN, R., and G. TCHOBANOGLOUS

    1968   Removal of nitrogen and phosphorus. Presented 23rd Purdue Industrial Waste Conf., Purdue Univ., Lafayette, Ind. May 8.

ENGEL, L.

    1961   The Sea. Time-Life Books (New York). 190 pp.

GOSNER, K. L.

    1971   Guide to Identification of Marine and Estuarine Invertebrates: Cape Hatteras to the Bay of Fundy. Wiley (New York). 693 pp.

GOTTO, R. V.

    1969   Marine Animals: Partnerships and Other Associations. American Elsevier (New York). 96 pp.

HARDY, A. H.

    1956   The Open Sea: The World of Plankton. Collins (London). 335 pp.

HERALD, E. S.

    1961   Living Fishes of the World. Doubleday (New York). 304 pp.

HUIBERS, D. T. A., R. McNABNEY, and A. HALFON

    1969   Ozone treatment of secondary effluents from wastewater treatment plants. Wat. Poll. Contr. Adm. Publ., PB 187 758. 62 pp.

JAHN, T. L., and L. R. KUHN

    1932   The life history of *Epibdella melleni* MacCallum 1927, a monogenetic trematode parasitic on marine fishes. *Biol. Bull.*, **62**:89–111.

JOHNSON, R. L., F. J. LOWES, JR., R. M. SMITH, and T. J. POWERS

    1964   Evaluation of the use of activated carbons and chemical regenerants in treatment of waste water. PHS Publ. No. 999-WP-13. 48 pp.

KING, J. M., and W. E. KELLEY

    1972   Air-lift pumps and the efficiency of undergravel filters. *Sea Scope* (Aquarium Systems, Inc.), **2**:5.

LAGLER, K. F., J. E. BARDACH, and R. R. MILLER

    1962   Ichthyology. Wiley (New York). 545 pp.

LANE, F. W.

    1960   Kingdom of the Octopus. Sheridan House (New York). 300 pp.

MACGINITIE, G. E., and N. MACGINITIE

    1949   Natural History of Marine Animals. McGraw-Hill (New York). 473 pp.

MARISCAL, R. N.

    1972   Behavior of symbiotic fishes and sea anemones. *In* Behavior of Marine Animals (Vol. 2), H. E. Winn and B. L. Olla (Eds.). Plenum (New York). 503 pp.

MARLER, P., and W. J. HAMILTON III
    1966   Mechanisms of Animal Behavior. Wiley (New York). 771 pp.

MIKLOSZ, J. C.
    1970   Biological filtration. *Marine Aquarist*, 1:22-29.

NIGRELLI, R. F.
    1936   Life-history of *Oodinium ocellatum*. *Zoologica*, 21:129-164 (9 plates).

NIGRELLI, R. F.
    1969   Parasites and diseases. *In* The Encyclopedia of Marine Resources. F. E.
            Firth (Ed.). Van Nostrand Reinhold (New York). 740 pp.

NIGRELLI, R. F., and G. D. RUGGIERI, S.J.
    1965   Studies on virus diseases of fishes. Spontaneous and experimentally
            induced cellular hypertrophy (lymphocystis disease) in fishes of the New
            York Aquarium, with a report of new cases and an annotated biblio-
            graphy (1874–1965). *Zoologica*, 50:83-96 (10 plates).

NIGRELLI, R. F., and G. D. RUGGIERI, S.J.
    1966   Enzootics in the New York Aquarium caused by *Cryptocaryon irritans*
            Brown, 1951 (=*Ichthyophthirius marinus* Sikama, 1961), a histophagous
            ciliate in the skin, eyes and gills of marine fishes. *Zoologica*, 51:97–102
            (7 plates).

NIGRELLI, R. F., and H. VOGEL
    1963   Spontaneous tuberculosis in fishes and in other cold-blooded vertebrates
            with special reference to *Mycobacterium fortuitum* Cruz from fish and
            human lesions. *Zoologica*, 48:131-144 (6 plates).

OMMANNEY, F. D.
    1963   The Fishes. Time-Life Books (New York). 192 pp.

PAULEY, G. B., and R. E. NAKATANI
    1967   Histopathology of "gas-bubble" disease in salmon fingerlings. *J. Fish.
            Res. Bd. Canada*, 24:867-871.

PETERSON, E. J., and R. C. ROBINSON
    1967   A meal-gelatin diet for aquarium fishes. *Prog. Fish-Cult.*, 29:170–171.

RANDALL, J. E.
    1968   Caribbean Reef Fishes. TFH Publications (Jersey City). 318 pp.

REICHENBACH-KLINKE, H., and E. ELKAN
    1965   The Principal Diseases of Lower Vertebrates. Academic Press (New
            York) 600 pp.

RUBIN, E., R. EVERETT, JR., J. J. WEINSTOCK, and H. M. SCHOEN
    1963   Contaminant removal from sewage plant effluents by foaming. PHS
            Publ. No. 999–WP–5. 56 pp.

RUGGIERI, G. D. (S.J.), R. F. NIGRELLI, P. M. POWLES, and D. G. GARNETT

1970　Epizootics in yellowtail flounder, *Limanda ferruginea* Storer, in the Western North Atlantic caused by *Ichthyophonus*, an ubiquitous parasitic fungus. *Zoologica*, **55**:57–62 (10 plates).

SINDERMANN, C. J.

1970　Principal Diseases of Marine Fish and Shellfish. Academic Press (New York). 369 pp.

SMITH, F. G. W.

1971　Atlantic Reef Corals. Univ. Miami Press (Miami). 164 pp.

SNIESZKO, S. F, and H. R. AXELROD (Eds.).

1971　Bacterial Diseases of Fishes (Book 2A). TFH Publications (Jersey City). 145 pp.

SPOTTE, S. H.

1970　Fish and Invertebrate Culture: Water Management in Closed Systems. Wiley (New York). 145 pp.

TODD, D. E. (Ed.)

1970　The Water Encyclopedia. Water Information Center (Port Washington, NY). 559 pp.

TRUSSELL, R. P.

1972　The percent un-ionized ammonia in aqueous solutions at different pH levels and temperatures, *J. Fish. Res. Bd. Canada*, **29**: 1505–1507.

WOLF, F. A., and F. T. WOLF

1949　The Fungi (Vol. 1). Wiley (New York). 538 pp.

Index